WITHDRAWN

For Reference

Not to be taken from this room

AMERICAN CITY CHRONOLOGY SERIES

ATLANTA
A CHRONOLOGICAL & DOCUMENTARY HISTORY

1813-1976

Compiled and Edited by
GEORGE J. LANKEVICH

Series Editor
HOWARD B. FURER

1978
OCEANA PUBLICATIONS, INC.
Dobbs Ferry, New York

*To Anne and John
but especially for Anna*

Library of Congress Cataloging in Publication Data
Main entry under title:

Atlanta: a chronological & documentary history,
1813-1976.

(American cities chronology series)
Bibliography: p.
Includes index.
SUMMARY: A chronology of events in the history of
Atlanta from 1813 to 1976 with a selection of pertinent
documents.
1. Atlanta — History — Chronology. 2. Atlanta —
History — Sources. [1. Atlanta — History]
I. Lankevich, George J., 1939-
F294.A857A87   975.8'231'04   77-25048
ISBN 0-379-00618-9

© Copyright 1978 by Oceana Publications, Inc.

All rights reserved. No part of this publication may be produced or transmitted in any form or by any means, electronic or mechanical, including photocopy, recording, xerography, or any information storage and retrieval system, without permission in writing from the publisher.

Manufactured in the United States of America

TABLE OF CONTENTS

EDITOR'S FOREWORD v

CHRONOLOGY
    From Terminus to Gate City of the South, 1813-1857 1
    War and Reconstruction, 1858-1870 11
    The Phoenix, 1871-1915 22
    A Generation of Challenge, 1916-1936 47
    The Hartsfield Era, 1937-1961 56
    Metropolis of the South, 1962 to the present 66

DOCUMENTS
    Early Atlanta, 1839 79
    Railroads Come to Atlanta, 1845 81
    Atlanta Begins to Grow, 1847 83
    Morality Triumphant, 1851 86
    The Minute Man Association, 1860 89
    Sherman Takes Atlanta, 1864 91
    Atlanta Begins to Rebuild, 1865 95
    Atlanta: The Phoenix, 1871 97
    Atlanta's Black Population, 1881 99
    The New South, 1886 102
    The "Atlanta Compromise", 1895 105
    W.E.B. DuBois on Black Education in Atlanta, 1905 109
    The Riot of 1906 112
    Segregation in Atlanta, 1908 114
    The Lords of Coca-Cola, 1910 117
    Zoning in Atlanta, 1922 119
    The Viaduct System, 1929 121
    The Atlanta Housing Authority, 1938 123
    The End of an Era, 1961 125
    A New Mayor for Atlanta, 1962 130
    The Challenge of the Seventies, 1970 134
    The Future of Atlanta, 1974 137

BIBLIOGRAPHY 139

NAME INDEX 151

EDITOR'S FOREWORD

Will American cities be able to meet the challenges of the twentieth century? Can they halt the encroachment of urban blight and reverse its processes? Are the central cities of our nation fated to become bankrupt black ghettos surrounded by affluent and exclusive white suburbs? Will carefully constructed interracial coalitions be able to solve, or even adequately define the terrifying problems with which our metropoli are concerned? This litany of harsh questions is well known to the urbanologist and, increasingly, is at least the rhetorical concern of our national leadership. However, the seeming reluctance of the nation to respond has often occasioned dire forecasts and reduced many observers to despondency.

Yet in the uplands of northern Georgia, Atlanta, a capital which has always thrived on challenge and grown in adversity, is bravely facing the imposing agenda of urban problems. Just as Manchester in Great Britain and Chicago and Los Angeles in America were representative cities of their time, so Atlanta is today the "shock city" of our age. Modern Atlanta is blatantly new; it seems to have leaped from the architect's board into reality. Construction projects valued in the billions of dollars are underway; John Portman's Peachtree Center complex alone is expected to cost almost a billion dollars. The city has suddenly emerged as the third largest convention center in the nation, and five professional sports teams have been located there since 1965. Georgia's capital remains today, as it has been for a century, the distribution and communication center of the South. Atlantans inform the visitor that when Southerners die, whether their destination be heaven or hell, they change planes in the "Gate City."

Yet despite its affluence Atlanta is not immune from the problems that our cities must solve. Will this city, girded by white suburbs and with a stagnant core population, truly become a regional metropolis of 2,000,000 people by 1983? Will its business community, which has long guided the affairs of Atlanta, be willing to serve a central city that is more than half black and which is governed by black leaders? Can the familiar urban problems of housing decay, demands for better services, lack of adequate public transportation, drug abuse and racial tensions be solved there? These questions cannot yet be fully answered. We can be certain, however, that Atlanta is willing to make an attempt. In making the effort, the modern city will greatly benefit from the virtues and talents already displayed in her unique history. Few American cities would as willingly accept the challenge of the 1970's, or be as well prepared to do so, as does Atlanta.

George J. Lankevich
Bronx Community College

CHRONOLOGY

FROM TERMINUS TO GATE CITY OF THE SOUTH

1813-1814	Lieutenant George R. Gilmer heads a twenty-two man force which erects a fort at the "Standing Peachtree," where the Chattahoochee River receives Peachtree Creek.
1816	The Cherokee Indians win a lacrosse game from the Creeks and claim the lands of the Atlanta area.
1821	January 18. The Creeks cede all their central Georgia lands to the United States by signing the Treaty of Indian Springs.
1822	May. Samuel Mitchell obtains land title to much of the Atlanta area.
	December 9. Dekalb County is created by the Georgia legislature.
1825	A U.S. Postal Office, run by J.M.C. Montgomery, services the area around "Standing Peachtree" Village.
1826	A state survey decides that railroads, and not canals, can best develop the lands of north-central Georgia.
1827	November 15. The Creeks, by the second Treaty of Indian Springs, cede their remaining Georgia lands to the federal government.
1829	July. Gold is discovered on Cherokee lands in Georgia. This development, combined with the coming to power of of the Jackson Administration, assures a harsher Indian policy by the federal government.
1832	March 3. The Supreme Court decides <u>Worcester v. Georgia</u>, and declares invalid Georgia's policy toward the Cherokee. President Jackson declines to enforce the decision.
1833	Atlanta's first permanent settler, Hardy Ivy, most probably builds his homestead during the spring of this year
	December. The Georgia legislature charters three railroad companies; within thirteen years their tracks will converge at Atlanta.
1834	October. J. Edgar Thompson is hired as Chief Engineer of the Georgia Railroad.

1835	Spring. Charner Humphries constructs a two-story whitewashed tavern to service travelers.
	June. Humphries' Whitehall Inn is named a federal post office.
	December 23. Cherokee leader John Ridge signs the New Echota Treaty; he cedes all tribal lands to the United States for $5,000,000 and a western reservation.
1836	July 4. In Knoxville, Tennessee, a meeting of railroad promoters declares the necessity of a line to link northern Georgia with the midwest.
	December 21. The state legislature charters the Western and Atlantic Railroad, which intends to link Georgia with Chattanooga.
1837	May 12. Colonel Stephen Long begins a Western and Atlantic route survey. By September, his assistant, Albert Brisbane, sets the stake for Terminus, the end of the proposed line. The site selected, in Land Lot 78 of DeKalb County, is some 1,050 feet above sea level and eight miles from the Chattahoochee River.
1838	May 24. The army begins forceful relocation of Georgia's remaining Cherokees. The evictees begin the "trail of tears" westward, a journey that will cost some 4,000 Indian lives.
1839	Spring. John Thrasher arrives in Terminus and opens a general store. Business proves so poor that he leaves within eighteen months.
	June 22. John Ridge and two other men are murdered by dissident Cherokees who condemn the sale of tribal lands.
1841	The Western and Atlantic, having completed survey and grading preparations, begins laying rails; a depot is begun in Terminus.
1842	July 11. Although "in a perfect state of nature," Terminus, with only thirty persons in six buildings is officially designated the southeastern end of Western and Atlantic track. Samuel Mitchell donates five acres for public buildings and railroad yards.

CHRONOLOGY 3

August 17. Julia Carlisle, whose parents arrived only in June, is born in Marietta and becomes Terminus' first baby. Settlers begin to call their town Marthasville to honor the daughter of Georgia's governor.

December 24. The locomotive <u>Florida</u>, having been hauled by mules some sixty miles from Madison, makes a twenty mile trip to Marietta on W & A tracks. Regular train service does not begin for another three years.

1843

Spring. Several new families, including that of Thomas Kile, arrive after purchasing lots at a Georgia land sale.

December 23. A Georgia railroad survey done by Lemuel P. Grant is completed to Terminus.

December 29. The legislature grants a charter to Terminus, now renamed Marthasville. A five-man commission is appointed to govern the settlement.

1844

February-April. Although stationed in Marietta, Lieutenant William Sherman often rides over the Marthasville territory he will conquer twenty years later.

August. Jonathan Norcross opens a sawmill which supplies board to the growing town and cuts railroad ties. John Thrasher returns to Marthasville, a town which now has fifteen buildings and a dozen families.

1845

March 1. Marthasville, a rough railroad town, elects five new commissioners, but they fail to establish law and order or even to collect taxes.

May 31. George Washington Collier purchases a lot and opens a grocery, which will serve as Atlanta's first post office (1846).

June. A combination school/church is constructed and five denominations agree to share its facilities.

July. The town begins to call itself Atlanta, a name suggested by J. Edgar Thompson.

September 15. The first Georgia Railroad train arrives and opens up trade with Augusta.

Fall. Doctor Joshua Gilbert arrives; he is Atlanta's first physician.

Reverend John Barry celebrates Atlanta's first Catholic mass.

November 13. John C. Calhoun, chairman of the Southeastern Convention meeting in Memphis, predicts greatness for a town "where railroads unite"-- Atlanta.

December 15. Western and Atlantic tracks are completed.

December 26. The legislature approves a change of name, and Marthasville becomes Atlanta. Its government, however, remains an ineffective commission.

1846

April 24. Samuel Mitchell donates additional lands to Atlanta for use by the Macon and Western Railroad.

Spring. The Atlanta Hotel, financed by the Georgia Railroad and run by Dr. Joseph Thompson, opens for business.

July 14. The Luminary, Atlanta's first true newspaper, is published by Joseph Baker. A Whig newspaper, the Enterprise, publishes in August. No fewer than thirty-one papers and periodicals will be published in Atlanta before 1860.

August 1. The Georgia Agricultural Fair is held at Stone Mountain, outside Atlanta.

September 4. The Macon and Western becomes the third railroad to enter Atlanta; service begins on its 101 miles of track in October.

1847

April 13. Masonic Lodge #59 holds its first meeting; it is chartered on October 26.

June 10. The Atlanta Sabbath School opens.

Summer. Reverend John Hunt organizes an Episcopal congregation. However, the town is still dominated by the rowdy elements of "Slabtown," "Murrell's Row" and "Snake Nation," where the railroad men drink and wench.

July 2. The Southern Miscellany relocates its publishing plant in Atlanta.

November 8. William White opens a high school in the former Angier's Academy. Almost all Atlanta education for twenty-five years is privately provided.

December 29. Georgia charters the city of Atlanta and defines its borders as a one mile circle around the Depot mile marker. A mayor and six man council are given the task of bringing law and order to the rowdy community.

1848

January 8. The first Presbyterian congregation is formed.

January 29. The first city election is held at "Kile's Corner," a combination grocery/saloon. Two hundred fifteen men choose Moses Formwalt, a tinsmith and saloonkeeper, as Atlanta's first mayor.

February 2. The first meeting of the Atlanta City Council is held and the installation of wooden sidewalks and a ban on Sunday business are approved. J.O. and P.C. McDaniel soon erect Atlanta's first block of brick stores.

March. The Methodists dedicate Wesley Chapel, an outgrowth of the Union Sabbath School.

Atlanta becomes part of the Roman Catholic Diocese of Savannah.

May 28. Saint Philip's Episcopal Church is dedicated.

July 3. Mayor Formwalt appoints a nine-member board of Health led by Dr. Gilbert.

July 5. The First Baptist Church (organized January 1st) is dedicated by Minister D.G. Daniel.

September 3. Judge Francis Cone assaults Alexander Stephens with a knife in the Atlanta Hotel, but Stephens recovers.

November. A. Leyden opens the Atlanta Machine Works.

The city clerk is dismissed for his refusal to report city receipts from fines and license fees.

1849

January 17. Benjamin Bomar is inaugurated mayor; he represents churchgoers who hope for better law enforce-

January 18. The post of city marshal is created to help Atlanta cope with the "rowdy" party of transient railroad workers and saloonkeepers.

February 7. The council approves a tax of thirty cents on each $100 worth of property; few dollars are actually collected.

April 14. Atlanta issues its first bonds, $500 units payable in six months.

May. The Macon and Western Branch Telegraph office goes into operation.

Spring-Summer. A Methodist revival sweeps the Atlanta area and incidentally increases the town's population.

June 1. The Southern Miscellany, a newspaper published sporadically since 1847 and purchased by a group of businessmen led by Jonathan Norcross, begins publication as the Atlanta Intelligencer with J. Baker as the editor.

December 1. The Western and Atlantic completes 138 miles of track to Chattanooga.

1850

January 23. Atlanta's new mayor, William Buell, is inaugurated. The Seventh Census estimates city population at 2,572 with almost 500 slaves.

March 1. The council approves a one dollar tax on each slave sold at the Alabama Street Slave Pen.

April 10. The city pledges $1,000 and a ten-acre lot to the Southern Agricultural Association, which reciprocated by holding its August fair in Atlanta.

April 15. Atlanta has its first fire; arson is committed on Alabama Street to cover the robbery of the Georgia Railroad office. The incident proves the necessity for a fire company

June. The city buys six acres for use as a municipal graveyard; the site is later named Oakland Cemetery.

December. The mayoral compaign is a contest between the "Free and Rowdy" party and the "Moral" party led by Jonathan Norcross. Norcross defeats Leonard Simpson.

CHRONOLOGY

1851

January 23-March. After his inauguration, Norcross brings law and order to Atlanta with the help of a business/vigilante coalition. A new jail is constructed in February and a raid by "White Cap" reformers burns "Snaketown" to the ground. Prostitutes are expelled from the city.

February 13. Reverend James O'Neill becomes the first pastor of the Catholic Church of the Immaculate Conception.

March 24. A volunteer fire company, Atlanta #1, is organized; it is incorporated on April 4.

July 29-31. Nine men are arrested to prevent a suspected slave insurrection.

Summer-Fall. Typhoid strikes Atlanta -- it recurs in 1852 -- for one of the few times in city history.

December. G.T. Gibbs is elected mayor of Atlanta.

1852

January 26. Mrs. T.S. Ogilby opens Atlanta's first music school.

January 27. The Bank of Atlanta is organized with a capitalization of $300,000, but no one buys its stock.

May 21. Slaves are required to have written permission for possessing liquor; the penalty for illegal possession is thirty-nine lashes.

July 4. The First Presbyterian Church is dedicated by Rev. John Wilson.

September 18. The Union Democrats, led by Howell Cobb, meet in Atlanta and decide not to bolt the Democratic Party in favor of the Southern Rights movement.

1853

January 17. John T. Mims becomes mayor of Atlanta after defeating incumbent Gibbs. He soon purchases land for a city hall, authorizes Edward Vincent to draw the first city map, and begins a system of poor relief.

January 28. A three-man police department is authorized by the council. A fire department is established in July.

February. The Atlanta and LaGrange Railroad reaches LaGrange.

March 25. Oil burning street lights are approved. Citizens are obligated to supply the oil for nighttime illumination and the city soon experiments with gas lights.

July. A tempory hospital for smallpox victims opens at the Fair Grounds.

Fall. The Holland Free School opens, and Joseph Winship organizes a machine foundry which he opens early in 1854.

September 24. Bids are received for construction of an Atlanta city hall designed by Columbus Hughes.

Atlanta's new railroad depot opens.

October 29. Mayor Mims announces his resignation and leaves Atlanta for Texas.

November 12. William Markham is designated to fill the unexpired portion of Mims' term.

November 28. Atlantans, led by William H. Butt, petition the legislature to declare Atlanta the new capital -- the effort fails.

December 20. Fulton County is set off from DeKalb, and Atlanta is designated the new county's seat.

1854

January. William H. Butt is elected mayor. The growing city, population 6,025, is divided into five wards.

February 3. The night police force is doubled to six officers.

February 18. The Georgia Western Railroad is chartered.

March 3. The council bans hogs from Atlanta's streets, approves creation of a gas lighting system, orders the mayor to create a city seal, and agrees that a new effort be made to transfer the state capital to Atlanta.

May 2. Ex-President Millard Fillmore is feted at the Atlanta Hotel.

June 30. The council grants newly organized Atlanta Medical College the privilege of holding lecture sessions in city hall.

August. The *Examiner* publishes as Atlanta's first daily newspaper. Only one week later, the *Intelligencer* becomes a daily.

September 1. The Second Baptist Church is formed when nineteen members secede from the First Church to seek a liberalized theology with more music. The new congregation worships in city hall until they construct their church. The Trinity Methodist Episcopal Church opens this month.

October 17. A Grand Ball commemorates the formal opening of city hall.

November. The Trout House receives its first guests.

December. Growing Atlanta can boast this year of opening its first fire station, macadamizing its first streets and again supressing the gambling interests of "Snaketown."

1855

January 8. The Atlanta Select School for young ladies is opened.

January 17. Allison Nelson defeats Know-Nothing Ira McDaniel for the mayoralty, 425-415.

February 16. A license for theatrical performances at the Athanaeum Theatre is granted to William Crisp, "the South's most accomplished Shakespearean actor."

March-April. After long debate, the council approves a city gas works, and agrees to purchase 40 per cent ($20,000) of the stock in William Helme's proposed operation.

June 21. The cornerstone for Atlanta Medical College is set, and the college graduates its first class on September 1.

The *Atlanta Medical and Surgical Journal* begins publication this year.

July 6. Mayor Nelson resigns after the council reduces a

sentence of his mayor's court.

July 20. John Glenn becomes mayor for the remainder of 1855.

September. Atlanta hosts the Georgia Agricultural Society Fair.

October. The Bank of Atlanta, functioning since 1853 under Samuel Higginson, survives its third run of the year.

December 25. Atlanta's first gas lamps are illuminated. A perpetual light, honoring the traditional South and the Confederacy, still shines in its lamppost in present day Atlanta.

1856

January 25. William Ezzard is elected mayor of Atlanta.

February 16. The Atlanta Gas Light Company is incorporated.

March 5. Atlanta holds a rally supporting southern interests in Kansas. An Emigrant Society is organized on August 4.

The legislature charters the Air Line Railroad. It also approves Atlanta's first city court and frees the mayor from service as a judge.

March 6. The Bank of Fulton, capitalized at $125,000 is incorporated.

June 3. The council denies as "unwise" a request by a black man to open an "ice cream saloon."

Summer. Richard Peters presides over the largest flour mill in the South, Thomas West opens the city's first "soda water" factory, and the council purchases 3,000 shares of stock in a bridge over the Chattahoochee River.

October 2. A Know-Nothing rally honoring Fillmore is marred when a man falls to his death from a flagpole.

December 10. Mechanics Fire Company #2 is granted a charter.

1857

January 6. Atlanta authorizes purchase of $100,000 in

CHRONOLOGY 11

Air Line Railroad stock.

January. William Ezzard is re-elected mayor of Atlanta.

June. Memphis' mayor labels Atlanta "Gate City of the South."

August-December. Atlanta weathers the financial panic quite easily, but the newly established Atlanta Rolling Mills is forced to suspend operation.

The first YMCA is established.

WAR AND RECONSTRUCTION

1858

January 1. Louis Schofield and William Markham reorganize the Rolling Mills and make it into the most efficient steel producer in the South. The plate they produce will ultimately armor the Merrimac.

January 8. The "Gate City Guard," Atlanta's most famous military organization, is formed.

January. Luther Glenn is elected mayor; his reforms include making ward representatives responsible for city services.

March 5. An additional purchase of $100,000 in Air Line bonds is authorized by the council. The council also receives a petition from Atlanta's mechanics protesting the use of slave labor in industrial plants.

May. The Atlanta Council refuses its promised support to the Air Line Railroad.

The Hiberian Society is organized to aid Irish immigrants in Atlanta.

November. Governor Joseph Brown proposes a statewide system of education for "free white children," but the legislature refuses to act.

1859

January 23. Glenn is re-elected mayor and his Inaugural promises reduction of the large city debt and better police protection.

February 15. Tallulah Fire Company #3 is organized.

February 22. The <u>Southern Confederacy,</u> a newspaper edited by James P. Hambleton, appears.

Local slave dealers protest outside competition and demand higher city license fees for slave traders.

April. The Georgia census reports a city population of 11,500; an Atlanta City Directory is published.

May 20. The council orders that free blacks post bonds of $200 to live in Atlanta; failure to do so makes them liable to indenture.

August 11. Construction begins on a new Masonic hall.

November 28. Hook and Ladder Company #1 is organized.

1860

January 20. William Ezzard becomes mayor for the third time but presides over a divided city. Leading citizens, like Markham and Norcross, flaunt their Union sentiments while other merchants demand an embargo on trade with all northern Abolitionists.

February 24. A merchants' meeting chaired by Norcross asks that Atlanta be designated a United States port of entry and that discriminatory railroad freight rates favoring Savannah and Charleston be ended.

March 4. The Central Presbyterian Church is dedicated.

March 8. Atlanta's four fire companies merge into one organization.

April 18. Atlanta's oldest Union, Typographers #48, is chartered.

April. Georgia Conservatives defeat a call for secession and union with Mexico. However, the Knights of the Golden Circle, who advocate the extension of slavery to Latin America, remain influential in Atlanta.

June 24. The new Masonic Hall is dedicated; it will be destroyed by fire on May 1, 1866.

CHRONOLOGY

August 16. Atlanta repeals its subscription of bonds in the Air Line Railroad.

October 30. Stephen A. Douglas speaks in Atlanta and defends the Union.

October 31. The Atlanta Minute Men Association is organized to defend states rights and work for secession from "Federal power wielded by a Black Republican Administration."

November 9. In the presidential election, Atlanta votes 1,070 for Bell, 835 for Breckinridge and only 335 for Douglas.

December 22. A fifteen-gun salute honors South Carolina's secession and Atlantans burn Lincoln in effigy.

December. The U.S. census reports an Atlanta population of 9,554.

1861

January 2. Fulton County elects three delegates to the State Secession Convention, among them Luther Glenn.

January 3. Atlanta organizes the Georgia Volunteers, even as an earthquake rocks the city at 4:40 P.M.

January 17. Jared Whitaker is elected mayor, defeating Ezzard in a bitter contest by 695-452.

January 19. Georgia becomes the fourth state to secede from the Union.

February 4. A citizens meeting endorses a proposed southern convention in Atlanta, but despite the city's dream, the confederate capital will not be located in the "Gate City."

February 16. A reception honoring Jefferson Davis is held at the Trout House.

March. The Gate City Guardian announces its new name, The Southern Confederacy.

March 12. Alexander Stephens is feted at the Atlanta Hotel.

April 1. Captain William Ezzard leads the Gate City Guard to war and garrison duty at Pensacola.

April 19. The Atlanta Committee of Public Safety is formed to care for soldiers' families.

June 3. A "Bank Convention" meets in Atlanta to deal with confederate financial problems.

July 5. Atlanta becomes the headquarters of the Georgia Military Affairs Committee.

August. Eleven companies of Atlanta/Fulton County volunteers are already in confederate service.

November 25. Mayor Whitaker resigns to become Georgia's commissary general; Thomas Lowe completes his term.

1862

January 15. James Calhoun becomes mayor of an Atlanta destined to serve as the major supply and distribution center for the confederacy.

April 11-12. James Andrews and his Union "raiders" seize the locomotive <u>General</u>, and race toward Chattanooga and the North. They are captured five miles short of their goal by confederate forces on the <u>Texas</u>.

June 7. Andrews is hanged on Peachtree Street; seven other "raiders" die on June 18. The city is declared a military post, and all liquor sales are restricted.

Summer. Atlanta's fair grounds become a hospital area for smallpox cases and confederate wounded.

August 11. General B. Bragg declares martial law in Atlanta.

August 16. Mayor Calhoun is named civilian governor of the city, but rejects the title.

September 3. The right of <u>habeus corpus</u> is suspended in Atlanta.

October 16. All conscripts between the ages of eighteen and forty-five are called to arms.

CHRONOLOGY

December 3. Calhoun is re-elected mayor. The first Wednesday of December becomes the new date for Atlanta's municipal election.

December 26. A smallpox hospital is ordered built to service the many cases of the disease among Confederate troops. A vaccination campaign is planned for 1863.

1863

February 13. The city council approves the creation of a secret police force.

March 22. Colonel Lemuel P. Grant is ordered to fortify Atlanta, clearly the distribution center of the Confederacy. Its hospitals care for 80,000 wounded soldiers during the war.

April 17. The sale of liquor is prohibited within city limits.

July 31. The city police form themselves into a para-military company.

September-October. Atlanta receives thousands of Confederate wounded from the Chickamauga battlefield.

October 30. Grant's defensive preparations are completed.

November 6. Despite the war and continued smallpox, a gala ball is held honoring the "Confederate Soldier."

1864

April 22. Saint Lukes Episcopal Church is dedicated.

May 7. General William T. Sherman begins his Atlanta campaign; he wins the Battle of Resaca on May 15.

May 23. Mayor Calhoun orders all citizens to form military companies.

June 5-July 3. Sherman fights constant battles with General Joseph Johnston in the area of Kennesaw Mountain.

June 10. Atlanta observes a day of "fasting, humiliation, and prayer."

June 16. Funeral services for General Leonidas Polk are held in St. Luke's Church.

ATLANTA

July 15. Sherman crosses the Chattahoochee River.

July 17. General John B. Hood replaces Johnston as defender of Atlanta. In the next thirteen days Hood will lose 8,800 men, a fact which guarantees the loss of the city.

July 20. The Battle of Peachtree Creek is lost. Light shelling of Atlanta begins.

July 22. During the Battle of Atlanta, Confederate General William Walker and Union General James McPherson die.

July 28. The Battle of Ezra Church ends in a draw.

August 20. Union cavalry strike at Jamesboro, south of Atlanta, in an effort to isolate the city.

August 25. Sherman lifts the seige in an attempt to capture Hood's army.

August 31-September 1. The Battle of Jamesboro ends in Union victory, and the Confederates must evacuate Atlanta. Setting fire to their supplies, they leave the city to mob rule.

September 2. "Atlanta is ours and fairly won," writes Sherman, as his troops occupy the city surrendered by Mayor Calhoun.

September 7. Sherman orders all civilians to leave Atlanta; forced evacuation begins on September 12, after a ten day truce is negotiated with General Hood.

November 14-15. The Union army sets fire to Atlanta as it leaves for its "march to the sea." Only 400 structures remain as Sherman leaves a city "smouldering and in ruins." Father Thomas O'Reilly saves five churches by overawing Sherman's Irish troops, and the Atlanta Medical College is preserved by Dr. Noel D'Alvigney.

November 26. Luther Glenn takes command of Atlanta as Confederate troops re-occupy the devastated city.

December 7. Calhoun is elected mayor for the fourth time, but the city treasury contains only $1.64.

1865

December 10. The <u>Daily Intelligencer</u> again begins publication.

February 27. Reverend Henry Hornady opens a school in the basement of the First Baptist Church.

May 4. Colonel Glenn turns Atlanta over to the First Ohio Cavalry after confirmation of Confederate surrender is received; liquor sales are immediately prohibited.

May 16. The American flag is officially raised and then lowered to half-mast to honor President Lincoln who was assassinated a month earlier.

June 20. Mayor Calhoun issues $20,000 in bonds (25 cents to 10 dollar denominations) which circulate as currency.

June 24. A citizens' meeting, chaired by Calhoun, resolves to restore commercial ties with the North, deplores the assassination of Lincoln, and calls for "speedy restoration of all political and national relations."

June. The Atlanta branch of the Freedman's Bureau establishes food distribution centers, which aid the indigent for two years.

July 7. Brigadier General Felix Salm-Salm becomes Atlanta's military governor.

July 14. All city ordinances discriminating between black and white are repealed.

July 21. The Atlanta Post Office again begins to handle the U.S. mail.

September 2. Alfred Austell organizes the Atlanta National Bank, the first such institution in the South; it opens on December 19 and Austell remains its president until his death on December 7, 1881.

October 25. Georgia's State Convention, meeting in Atlanta, repeals secession and abolishes slavery.

November. Classes resume at Atlanta Medical College.

December. James E. Williams, less committed to a Union policy than Calhoun, is elected mayor.

1866

January 26. Doctor Eli Griffin takes charge of the smallpox hospital, but the continued presence of the disease forces the city to open two additional pesthouses. Vaccination is mandated, half-burned buildings are ordered razed, and by August the epidemic is halted.

March 9. The Atlanta Mining and Rolling Mill Company is incorporated.

April-October. Four building and loan associations are organized to aid rebuilding efforts.

April 12. The Board of Trade is re-organized by R.M. Clarke and W.M. Lowry.

April 15. The Atlanta Ladies Memorial Association is formed.

April 21. The Gas Works resumes operations.

April 26. The first Confederate Memorial Day is celebrated.

May 21. The National Hotel opens. In other business news, the Miller Stock Yards opens and soon makes Atlanta the mule and cattle center of the South.

June. The Concordia Association (German) is established.

August. Atlanta Medical College graduates twenty-three students.

September 15. Peachtree Street is again lighted by gas.

October 16. Atlanta's first steam pumper goes into operation against fires.

October 19. Atlanta voters approve (152 to 30) expanding city limits to a one and a half mile circle around Zero Milepost.

December 5. James Williams is re-elected mayor as Atlanta's population reaches 20,228. Twenty-two private schools service the city.

1867

March 4. Congress passes the Reconstruction Act and makes Atlanta headquarters of the Third Military District. A mass meeting of Atlanta citizens, orginally led by former Mayor Calhoun, signifies acceptance of the Reconstruction Act. However, dissidents later seize control of the session, and pass substitute resolutions supporting President Johnson and condemning the act.

March 15. Atlanta contributes $1,000 toward Chattanooga flood relief.

March 31. John Pope arrives to command the Third Military District, and is honored with a dinner on April 12.

April 29-May 2. The Grand Ladies Fair is held, and a fire alarm bell is purchased with its proceeds.

May. Morris Rich opens a dry goods store at 36 Whitehall Street.

June 17. The Hebrew Benevolent Congregation is organized.

June 30. The Young Man's Library Association is formed and holds its first meeting on August 19.

Summer. Samuel Inman opens a cotton brokerage business.

August 12. General Pope bans all newspapers not favoring Reconstruction.

September 20. When the Lincoln Memorial Association requests a donation from Atlanta, the city agrees to donate only after the association collects $750,000, a level it never reaches.

October 15. A new charter is granted to Atlanta University. Edmund Ware is named its president.

December. General Pope orders mayor Williams to remain in office for another year. Pope also oversees the Constitutional Convention (130 delegates, 22 blacks) which drafts a new state constitution, a task completed by March, 1868.

1868

January 13. George Meade, Pope's successor as military commander, removes Georgia's governor and treasurer for refusing to pay costs for the Constitutional Convention.

February 27. Atlanta is named Georgia's capital by the convention.

April 20-22. Despite Klan activities versus blacks, the constitution wins voter approval. Rufus Bullock is elected governor and takes office on July 22.

May. The Atlanta Bible Association is established.

June 16. The <u>Atlanta Constitution</u>, founded by Colonel Cary Styles, first publishes.

July 4. The Georgia legislature convenes in Atlanta. Foes of Reconstruction, among them Robert Toombs, Howell Cobb and Benjamin Hill, denounce its usurpations at the "Bush Arbor" meeting on July 23.

July 29. Benjamin Hill is sent to the U.S. Senate to fight Reconstruction.

August 14. The Atlanta Council agrees that H.I. Kimball's Opera House be renovated (at his expense) to serve as the state capitol.

City Engineer James Cooper completes a new map of Atlanta.

October. Moore's Business College opens with nine students.

November 3. Atlanta votes for Horatio Seymour, the Democratic candidate for president.

November 26. Ordinances are adopted that legalize black voting in Atlanta.

December 2. William Hulsey is elected mayor.

December 11. Atlanta's council affirms the purchase of $300,000 in Georgia Western Railroad stock.

1869

January 1. Atlanta officially becomes Georgia's fifth capital.

March 18. Georgia, which expelled all blacks from its legislature in September, 1868 now rejects the Fifteenth Amendment to the Constitution.

March 30. Atlanta purchases land which will become Oglethorpe Park.

April. A freight depot is opened by the Georgia Railroad.

June 28. The Georgia Railroad hires about 350 convicts to reconstruct its track.

Summer. Atlanta raises $30,000 to finance the relocation of Oglethorpe University in the city. The Freedman's Aid Society of the Methodist Episcopal Church organizes a coeducational school that becomes Clark College.

September 1. The cornerstone of a new Church of the Immaculate Conception, a Gothic structure designed by William H. Parkins, is set in place. Parkins designed many major structures as Atlanta is rebuilt from its ashes.

November 26. The council asks public support for a municipal school system. This request is necessary because the four Freedman's Bureau schools are educating more blacks than private schools are educating whites.

December 1. William Ezzard is elected mayor and the voters elect a council committed to free public education.

December 10. The twelve-member Atlanta Board of Education is named; it will construct a school system using a $100,000 bond issue voted in 1870.

December 22. Unrepentant and unreconstructed Georgia is returned to military rule.

1870

January 16. The Christian Church of Atlanta is dedicated.

January 24. Lawrence DeGive opens his new Opera House with the play Richelieu.

July 15. Georgia is readmitted to the Union after ratifying the Fifteenth Amendment (February 2).

September 1. The First Methodist Church, once Wesley Chapel, sets its cornerstone in place.

October 4. Oglethorpe University re-opens in Atlanta, but financial difficulties force it to close again in December, 1872.

October 17. The Kimball House Hotel, "finest in the South," is opened.

October 27. The John James Mansion, completed only last December, becomes the governor's mansion. It held the honor until 1921 and was razed in 1923.

December 7. Dennis F. Hammond, a radical, becomes mayor, and two blacks are elected to serve on his council. Atlanta's population has risen to 21,789 persons, occupying nine square miles. It is about to begin its reign as the South South's commercial center, despite the fact that one historian believes that 25 per cent of its population was Confederate widows.

THE PHOENIX

1871

April 3. The Robert E. Lee Fire Company #4 is organized.

April 24. The Atlanta Pioneer and Historical Society is formed with William Ezzard as its president.

May 29. Contracts are let for a $130,000 waterworks system. It will be completed by 1875 at a cost of $226,000.

June 14. Wesley Chapel becomes the First Methodist-Episcopal Church in the South.

July 1. The Atlanta Female Seminary opens for its first classes.

July 23. A rain and hail storm causes vast damage around Atlanta.

August 7. The Chamber of Commerce is organized by Major Benjamin Crane; it will demand that growing Atlanta be designated a U.S. port of entry.

September 8. Atlanta's first streetcar line, the West End Railway, is completed to the McPherson Barracks. The Union passenger station is also completed by the five rail systems that service Atlanta.

October 2. The Gate City Fire Company #5 is established.

CHRONOLOGY

October 23. Governor Rufus Bullock resigns and flees the state to avoid prosecution for corruption. Samuel Bard of the Daily True Georgian was instrumental in driving Bullock from office.

November 15. Bernard Mallon of Savannah is named first superintendent of the public schools.

December 6. John James is unaminously elected mayor.

Growing Atlanta boasts seven wards (the sixth formed in October, the seventh in December, 1871) and a movement to revise the charter begins to gain momentum.

1872

January 4. Atlanta is divided into four school districts.

January 14. The Marietta Street Railway goes into operation.

February 1. The Atlanta Public School System formally opens with twice the expected number of registrants.

February. Congress appropriates $100,000 for an Atlanta post office and federal court.

May 3. The Decatur Street Railway begins operation.

June. Trinity Methodist Church opens.

Ferdinand Wurm begins forty years of musical service to his city when he organizes Atlanta's first symphony orchestra.

August 8. The Ponce de Leon Street Railway becomes operative. Colonel George W. Adair has, within a year, created a municipal transit system.

August 22. The Atlanta Daily Herald, Henry Grady part owner and editor, first appears. It merges with the Constitution on February 14, 1876.

August 24. The Macon and Central lines merge to form the Central of Georgia Railroad.

October-November. Atlanta is swept by a spiritualist revival led by Annie C. Torrey.

November 8. The Citizens Bank of Georgia is incorporated.

December 4. Cicero C. Hammock is elected mayor.

December 31. Two high schools and seven grade schools are in operation, serving 2,075 students.

1873   January. The Atlanta Manufacturers Association is formed.

March 1. The Atlanta Turnverein Society is established.

March 30. A street railway begins operation on Taylor Street, and the McDonough Street line follows suit on May 26.

May 30. Atlanta appropriates funds to number all houses in anticipation of free mail delivery, to begin on July 1.

July. Thomas Jones becomes Atlanta's first chief of police.

August 26. The Air Line, fifth railroad to serve the city, opens direct rail trade with the North. Its passenger service begins on September 28.

August 28. A Catholic petition for separate schools supported by city funds is rejected.

September-December. Not a single Atlanta bank fails during the financial panic. Indeed, Atlanta continues to prosper as her cotton trade rises 25 per cent over 1872.

November. A revised city charter is sent to the legislature for approval.

December 3. Samuel B. Spencer is elected mayor.

December 10. Dedication ceremonies are held at the Church of the Immaculate Conception.

1874   January. Atlanta women organize the Benevolent Society.

February 15. The Whitehall Street Railway begins to operate.

February 28. The governor signs a revised city charter

which strengthens the mayor's office, creates a bicameral legislature of ten councilmen and three aldermen and limits Atlanta's debt capacity. Separate education, police and water boards are authorized and the city is redistricted into five wards.

March. The first board of police commissioners is elected.

April 26. A monument to the "Confederate Dead" is unveiled in Oakland Cemetery.

May 28. A petition requesting that Catholic teachers instruct Catholic students is denied by the city.

November. William H. Felton wins the first of three congressional terms during which he will represent the interests of small farmers against the "Atlanta ring" of Bourbon politicians.

December 4. Hammock is elected Atlanta's first two-year mayor.

1875

January. Hammock begins the restoration of Atlanta's credit and induces a New York brokerage house to accept 7 per cent city bonds.

March 1. A hurricane strikes the city; a whirlwind of a different order hits Atlanta as entrepreneur Joel Hurt arrives.

July 4. For the first time since 1860, Atlanta celebrates Independence Day. Citizens hear Alexander Stephens memorialize a "preeminently" southern holiday.

August 21. Ground is broken for the new U.S. post office.

September 11. After a decade of work, the municipal water system begins to operate.

October 21. James Calhoun, Atlanta's wartime mayor, dies.

November 15. The Markham Hotel is opened.

1876

January 8. The Atlanta Sanitary Commission is formed to deal with the problems of waste disposal.

February 21-24. Edwin Booth plays in Hamlet at DeGive's Theatre.

June. Atlanta University graduates its first class.

August. Hundreds flee an outbreak of yellow fever in Savannah; among the refugees sheltered by Atlanta is Joel C. Harris, who soon goes to work for the Constitution.

October 18. Captain Evan Howell buys the Constitution and adds Henry Grady to its staff.

November. The Rossini Club presents Balfe's Bohemian Girl.

November 5. Jonathan Norcross is defeated as the Republican candidate for governor.

December 6. N. L. Angier is elected mayor.

1877

January 1. Atlanta's city debt is $2,175,240. However, its establishment of credit in the New York City market has eased its financial burden.

January 25. Julius Brown reorganizes the Beethoven Society.

July 11. Georgia's Constitutional Convention meets in Atlanta under the leadership of Charles Jenkins. The delegates reduce Atlanta's statewide political power by adopting the county unit system of representation.

August 31. Atlanta's first Hebrew synagogue is dedicated (cornerstone set May, 1875).

September 22. Rutherford B. Hayes, touring to attract southern support for his administration, becomes the first incumbent president to visit Atlanta.

December 5. Georgia voters approve the new constitution and also decide that Atlanta will remain the state capital.

1878

October 1. A local weather station is established in the Kimball House Hotel.

December 4. William L. Calhoun, son of a former mayor, is elected mayor defeating James English, 2509 to 1898.

1879

January 29-31. General Sherman returns to the city he ordered burned; no incidents mar the visit, and Sherman predicts greatness for Atlanta.

July. Ex-governor Bulloch organizes the Atlanta Cotton Mills.

August. Major W.F. Slayton becomes superintendent of schools, a post he holds for the next twenty-eight years.

October 1. Atlanta issues $385,000 in 6 per cent bonds as the city strives to reduce the obligations incurred by previous high interest rates. Mayor Calhoun's administration will successfully carry out a policy of efficient debt management.

November 1. Doctor Thomas Powell opens Southern Medical College in Atlanta; its first class has sixty-four students.

1880

February 1. Chrisman Hall is dedicated on the campus of Clark University.

February 28. Saints Peter and Paul, Atlanta's second Catholic church, is opened.

May. The Sisters of Mercy open Atlanta's first hospital for the destitute sick, St. Joseph's Infirmary.

Summer. Rich's Dry Goods store relocates at 54 Whitehall Street, where it installs Atlanta's first plate glass windows.

October 28. Edward Atkinson of Boston, speaking in Atlanta, condemns waste in cotton processing procedures. Atlanta begins to plan a cotton exposition.

December 1. James English defeats H.I. Kimball and becomes mayor.

December. Joel Chandler Harris publishes <u>Uncle Remus: His Songs and Sayings</u>.

December 29. A six inch snowfall paralyzes the city for four days.

The U.S. Census reports Atlanta's population as 37,409, making it the largest city in Georgia. The city has 196 manufacturing establishments and seventeen miles of newly laid sewers, but the census reports that 50 per cent of the population has inadequate incomes.

1881

January. James English is inaugurated and pledges to expand Atlanta's economy. Under his administration the Georgia Pacific Railroad pushes west into the coal fields of Alabama, the city holds its first exposition, debt is reduced and gambling curbed.

February 16. Sarah Bernhardt plays in <u>Camille</u> at the opera house.

March. The Atlanta Hospital and Benevolent Home opens.

April 11. The Women's Baptist Home Mission Society opens a female seminary for black women -- the forerunner of Spelman Seminary.

September 3. The charter is amended to permit construction of a drainage system.

September 8. The West End Railway is opened to McPherson Barracks.

October 5-December 31. An international cotton exposition, the first world's fair held in the South, is held in Atlanta under the direction of H.I. Kimball. Its key exhibit among 1,113 is a model cotton factory.

November 18. General John Gordon drives the first spike for the Georgia Pacific Railroad.

December 31. Atlanta reports its best year for cotton trading; one hundred and thirty thousand bales are received, almost two thirds of them by the Inman Comapny.

1882

January 1. A three man board of sewers and streets and a five member board of health, take office.

March 4. The Exposition Cotton Mill Company is incorporated.

April-July. Smallpox breaks out in "Beaver Slide," a black

ghetto. Of 110 reported cases, 109 are blacks.

July 1. A paid fire department is organized under Chief Matthew Ryan. An electric alarm system of twenty-six boxes is immediately installed.

August 16. Senator Benjamin Hill dies at his home on Peachtree Street; twenty thousand Georgians march in his funeral cortege. Among Atlanta's new residents this year are lawyer Woodrow Wilson and black barber, later millionaire, Alonzo Herndon.

September. Joel Hurt organizes the Atlanta House Insurance Company.

October 15. First services are held in St. Philip's Episcopal Cathedral.

December 6. John Goodwin defeats E.J. Roach, 1,247 to 881, and becomes mayor.

1883

January. Goodwin is inaugurated and completes Mayor English's building programs; major street, sewer and park improvements mark his administration.

February 24. The Atlanta Journal is founded by Edward F. Hoge.

March. The Nine O'Clock German Club is founded, oldest social club in Atlanta.

March 27. Atlanta's Unitarian congregation, the Church of the Father, is organized.

April 16. The Capital City Club is organized by eighty-two business and social leaders. It is incorporated May 31.

May 17. Fulton County Courthouse is dedicated, and the city formally accepts a gift of one hundred acres for parks from Colonel L.P. Grant.

May 26. In order to accept Colonel Grant's gift, a park commission is named; Charles Roesch is hired to plan a municipal park.

August 12. The Kimball House burns down, and the Journal

scores a coup by printing Atlanta's first "extra."

October 5. The Atlanta Chamber of Commerce is incorporated.

December 18. Gammon Hall is dedicated on the campus of Clark University.

1884

January. Joseph Jacobs opens a drugstore, later an Atlanta landmark, on Peachtree Street.

Drilling begins on a 2,044 foot artesian well located at the five points intersection, the downtown hub, where Peachtree, Decatur and Marietta Streets meet Edgewood Avenue.

The Women's Industrial Union is organized to give a voice to textile workers and provide a retail outlet for their homemade goods.

November 5. The Sixth Ward is created and elects its first alderman in December.

November 7. In celebration of the election of Grover Cleveland, a mob led by Constitution editor Henry Grady invades the capital and forces the legislature to adjourn.

December 3. George Hillyer is elected mayor of Atlanta.

1885

January. The reorganized Winship Machine Company is rechartered.

January 16. The Chamber of Commerce first convenes in its new building.

April 30. The Kimball House formally reopens; it soon installs the first hydraulic elevator in Atlanta (1886). A new YMCA building also opens this year.

May 19-21. The National Commercial Convention is held in Atlanta.

July 1. William R. Joyner is elected fire chief, a post he holds for twenty-one years.

September 2. The cornerstone of the new capitol building is set.

October 15. The first class enters Morris Brown College.

November 14. Fulton County approves a prohibition law.

December. Atlanta has 12.5 miles of paved streets and 56.5 miles of curbed sidewalks. Its population is served by four streetcar companies, twelve schools and fifty-six churches. Its business community can use any of eight railroad lines or seven banks. Its cotton trade continues to grow with 170,225 bales received this year.

1886

March. Atlanta decides to build a combined refuse/storm sewer system whose construction will be supervised by a commissioner of public works (replacing the board of streets and sewers).

Spring. Mrs. Livingstone Mims and Miss Julia Bartlett organize the first Christian Science congregation in the South, but no church is built until 1899.

May 1. A statue of Benjamin Hill is unveiled in Atlanta, and the occasion sees the public reconciliation of Jefferson Davis with General James Longstreet.

May. John S. Pemberton makes the first "ideal brain tonic," a product that will become famous not as a headache remedy but as Coca-Cola, "Georgia-Champagne."

July 1. Saloons in Atlanta are forced to close under the prohibition amendment approved last November.

October. Atlanta is chosen as the site for a Georgia Institute of Technology.

Rockefeller Hall opens as the administrative building of Spelman Seminary.

November. A prison congress led by Sidney Root calls for an end to the convict leasing system, a reform not achieved until 1908.

December 21. Henry Grady, inspired by the presence of William Sherman, addresses the New England Society of New York on "The New South."

December 24. Joel Hurt organizes the Atlanta and Edgewood

	Street Railway Company which begins to build track toward the suburbs. Led by Hurt, it becomes the first electric rail system in the world to show a profit.
1887	January. J.T. Cooper, a moderate Prohibitionist, is inaugurated mayor of Atlanta.
	April 1. A charter is granted to the Gentleman's Riding Club; their clubhouse opens on October 8.
	June 1. The Atlanta Bridge and Axle Company is created.
	Hoke Smith purchases the <u>Atlanta Journal</u>.
	June 28. Pemberton registers Coca-Cola as a trademark. He will sell about 1,000 gallons of his former headache remedy this year.
	July-October. Led by Charles Collier, Atlanta organizes within 104 days an exposition to display the resources of the Piedmont area of the South.
	July 19. Atlanta swelters in 100-degree heat, its highest recorded nineteenth century temperature.
	October 1-10. Over 200,000 people visit Atlanta during the Piedmont Exposition.
	October 18. Grover Cleveland speaks at the Markham House Hotel.
	November. The city adopts a new seal, "Resurgens Atlanta," which depicts a phoenix rising from the flames of Sherman's destruction. Equally uplifting is a Fulton County vote which repeals its prohibition on liquor.
1888	January 16. The Atlanta Philosophical Association is organized.
	March 24. Gammon Theological Seminary is separated from Clark University when it obtains its own charter.
	April 14. Asa Candler and his associates buy control of Coca-Cola.
	April 28. The Atlanta Bar Association is incorporated.

CHRONOLOGY

August. Atlanta shelters the refugees who flee from an outbreak of yellow fever in Jacksonville.

September. "Dummy" steam engines are introduced by Metropolitan Street Railway Company.

September 3. The Georgia Conservatory of Music accepts its first class.

October. The Richmond Terminal Company purchases the Georgia Central for $12,000,000 and creates an 8,000 mile system of track.

October 7. The Georgia Institute of Technology opens.

December. John T. Glenn is elected mayor after a bitter contest on Prohibition. He pledges to control but not abolish the liquor traffic.

December 19. The Richmond Terminal Company leases the Georgia Pacific.

1889

February 1. Atlanta's streets are illuminated by electric lights.

March. George Gress, a transplanted New Yorker who is the the "lumber king of Georgia," buys a bankrupt circus, and donates its menagerie to Atlanta as a zoo for Grant Park.

Joel Hurt organizes the United Underwriters Insurance Company.

March 25. The Hebrew Orphans Home is dedicated.

May 4. Fort McPherson becomes a permanent U.S. Army Post.

Jasper Smith opens his "House that Jack Built," a curiosity covered with Biblical inscriptions.

June 15. The new state capitol, designed by Edbrooke and Burnham, and with a dome that soars 237 feet into the air, is completed. Formal dedication ceremonies are held on July 4.

August 21. Joel Hurt is the motorman as the first electric

trolleys run along Edgewood Avenue to Inman Park.

December. Henry Grady is elected president of the Jefferson Davis Memorial Association. On December 12, he lectures on "The Race Problem" to a Boston audience. Taken suddenly ill, he returns to Atlanta, where he dies on December 23.

1890

March 1. William B. Hartsfield, later Atlanta's greatest mayor, is born.

April 4. Atlanta adds forty-four acres to Grant Park.

June 15. The first class is graduated from Georgia Tech.

August 10. A children's "penny" campaign helps purchase an elephant, "Clio," for the zoo.

October 19. The Salvation Army opens its first mission in Atlanta.

November 23. John Beckwith, Episcopal bishop of Atlanta since 1868, dies.

December 3. William A. Hemphill is elected mayor.

Atlanta's population of 65,533 is 42.9 per cent black (28,098). In its nine square miles, Atlanta has one hundred miles of street railway, giving it the most complete rail system in America.

1891

January. The eighty-one acres of Maddox Park are acquired at a cost of $19,045.

April. President Benjamin Harrison and African explorer Henry Stanley visit Atlanta.

May 16. Joel Hurt organizes the Atlanta Consolidated Street Railway Company.

June 25. The Equitable Building, tallest and first fireproof building in the South, has its cornerstone set.

June-July. The Bradley-Osborn murder shocks Atlanta; Osborn is ultimately hanged.

July 9. The first train of the East Tennessee Railroad enters Atlanta.

September 6. The legislature creates Atlanta's first criminal court.

October. Barney Kleinbaker opens the Edgewood Avenue Theatre.

October 21. Henry Grady's daughter unveils a monument to his memory, designed by Alexander Doyle.

November 21. Agnes Scott College, the former Decatur Seminary, opens.

1892

January. Atlanta's electric light and power industry is consolidated by the Georgia Electric Light Company. New waterworks, drawing from the Chattahoochee River, will also be completed.

January 29. Asa Candler incorporates Coca-Cola in Georgia; he has held personal control of Coke since April, 1891.

February 10. Georgia's first college football game is held; Auburn 11, Georgia University 0.

February 22. The Battle of Atlanta, a cyclorama painting done by Milwaukee artists in 1885-1886, goes on display.

April 24. The first passenger train on the Georgia, Carolina, and Northern line reaches Atlanta and opens a second route to the North.

May 8. The first electric train runs on the "River Line" to the Chattahoochee River.

May 25. Grady Hospital is dedicated.

November 14. The Hotel Aragon opens on Peachtree Street.

December 6. John B. Goodwin is again elected mayor.

1893

January 18-19. A snowfall caves in the roof of the building that houses the Battle of Atlanta.

February 10. Laurence DeGive opens the Grand Opera House with Men and Women; the theatre immediately ranks as the South's finest showplace, having seats for 2,700 patrons and using electric lights.

March 5. Hoke Smith becomes secretary of the interior in Grover Cleveland's cabinet.

March 25. A central police station is completed. The department is run by a board of police commissioners led by the mayor.

The Forsyth Street Bridge opens for traffic.

July 25. Water from the Chattahoochee enters Atlanta for the first time, and the system is fully operative by September.

August. Atlanta offers itself as a "City of Refuge" to those fleeing yellow fever in Pensacola, Florida and Brunswick, Georgia.

August 14. The Chamber of Commerce suggests that bank certificates on cotton crop futures circulate as currency; Atlanta easily weathers the financial panic.

October. A second Baptist Church is dedicated, and suitable celebrations marks its fiftieth anniversary.

November. Leonard Wood organizes a team of "Yellow Jackets" at Georgia Tech; they defeat the University of Georgia in football, 22-6.

November 23. Annexation of the city of West End is approved, and it becomes the city's seventh ward.

December 12. C.B. Adams is awarded the first patent for aerial photography.

1894

February 10. Clark Howell is elected first president of the Atlanta Press Club.

April 26. The "Lion of Atlanta," modelled after the Lion of Lucerne, is unveiled in Oakland Cemetery to honor all Confederate dead.

June 18. The Southern Railway Company is organized by Samuel Spencer.

CHRONOLOGY

October. The American Street Railway Association convenes in Atlanta to study Hurt's extremely successful electric rail system.

November 3. Joseph Brown dies, and his body lies in state at the capitol.

1895   January. Porter King is sworn in as Atlanta's mayor; he had been elected without opposition the previous October.

April 29. The New Lyceum Theatre opens.

August. Lakewood Park opens -- for whites only.

September 18. Twenty-five thousand visitors jam the opening of the Cotton States and International Exposition. The one hundred days of the Expo will be famous for John Philip Sousa's "King Cotton March," the first woman's pavillion, and for a building for blacks in which Booker T. Washington presented his "Atlanta Compromise."

September 21. The Grand Army of the Republic joins the Confederate veterans to hold a common encampment at the exposition.

October 8. The Liberty Bell goes on display.

December. Atlanta University sponsors its first congress on Africa.

December 16. The legislature approves the annexation of West Atlanta.

1896   January 25. The Robert Burns Club of Atlanta is organized.

May 17. Fire destroys the Markham House, causing one death and $300,000 in damages.

May 26-27. W.E.B. DuBois of Atlanta University convenes the first conference on the urban black.

December 2. Charles A. Collier, planner of the Cotton Exposition, is elected mayor.

1897   January 1. The first football game between Atlanta's schools for blacks is held.

May 3. Atlanta purchases Fulton County courthouse for

conversion into a new city hall.

Bradford Gilbert's "flatiron" Georgia Savings Bank opens.

Clark Howell becomes editor in chief of the Constitution, and spokesman for the New South.

October 16. Expanding Atlanta annexes its northern suburbs and reduces its tax rate to only one and one quarter per cent per $100 of property.

1898

Atlanta Medical College and Southern Medical merge to create the Atlanta College of Physicians and Surgeons.

March 12. George Gress, who purchased the Battle of Atlanta cyclorama after it was damaged in 1893, presents the refinished masterpiece to the city.

April 21. War against Spain is declared. None of Atlanta's 3,000 volunteers will serve in combat duty.

July 20-23. Led by General John B. Gordon, 30,000 United Confederate veterans hold a reunion in Atlanta.

October 5. James G. Woodward, a printer, wins the primary election, and thus will become mayor of Atlanta in January.

December 4. The North Avenue Presbyterian Church is organized.

December 14-15. President William McKinley and his cabinet attend a Peace Jubilee in Atlanta to give thanks for victory in the war.

1899

February 13. Atlanta's lowest temperature, 8.5 degrees below zero is recorded.

April 2. A Christian Science church, in temporary quarters since 1886, is dedicated.

April 10. The Atlanta Athletic Club, one of the city's most prestigeous social organizations, opens a clubhouse.

Spring. The Mitchell Street Viaduct opens and connects the west side with downtown Atlanta.

CHRONOLOGY

May 6. The Carnegie Library is organized, with a donation of $145,000 from the steelmaster. Atlanta's public library today boasts 700,000 volumes in seventeen branches.

July 21. The right to bottle Coca-Cola is franchised; today over 1,100 plants around the world bottle Coke.

October 18. The Georgia State Fair is held in Atlanta.

October 26. A gala banquet honors Lt. Thomas Brumby, Admiral Dewey's flag officer at Manilla Bay.

1900

February 22. Ignace Jan Paderewski appears at the Grand Theatre.

Spring. Bottled Coke is first sold in America.

May 7. Thirty-four houses and several factories are destroyed by fire.

May. The Atlanta Rapid Transit Company is organized to compete with Hurt's Consolidated. When Hurt retires in 1901, his company is acquired by this combine.

Summer. Colonel J. C. Woodward opens the Georgia Military Academy.

September 29. The cornerstone of the Carnegie Library is set.

October 5. Livingstone Mims is elected mayor after campaigning against transit company abuses.

December. Atlanta ranks as the third city of the South behind New Orleans and Louisville; its population is 89,872 (39.8 per cent black).

1901

February 21. The Markham block is destroyed by fire at a loss of half a million dollars.

March 5. Eight entrepreneurs organize the Atlantic Steel Hoop Company, forerunner of Dixiesteel Corporation.

The Citizens Southern Banking Building opens on Broad Street.

June 3. A Confederate soldiers home opens, but burns down on September 30.

October 9. The Whitehall Street viaduct opens to more firmly unite the north and south sides of Atlanta.

November 6. The Lyceum Theatre burns down.

1902

January. The federal penitentiary, under construction since 1899, is completed.

January 27. H.M. Atkinson organizes the Georgia Railway and Electric Company and takes control of all street transit and electric steam power in Atlanta. Mayor Mims obtains concessions from the utility in return for Atlanta's grant of franchise privileges.

March 3. The Carnegie Library, designed by Ackerman and Ross (New York City), opens to the public.

May 17. In the "Pittsburgh Riot," a deranged sharpshooter kills five men before he is himself shot dead.

July 22. A monument to General William Walker (C.S.A.) is unveiled on Glenwood Avenue.

August 2. The Alhambra Hotel burns down.

August 4. The Atlanta News, a penny daily, first appears; John Graves is its editor.

October 1. Captain Evan Howell is elected mayor by winning the primary election.

November 3. Work begins on a new passenger terminal, Union Depot.

December 9. Fire in the business district destroys fourteen buildings worth $400,000.

1903

February 10. The Atlanta Terminal Company is organized to build a train shed.

March 15. The Lutheran Church of the Redeemer opens.

The Atlanta Independent, a black weekly that publishes until

1932, first appears.

1904 May 23. The council begins negotiations to purchase the 185 acres of Piedmont Park for use as a municipal recreation area; it is later the site for an annual arts festival.

August 3. Atlanta's Eighth Ward is approved; its area is largely that of the Piedmont acquisition.

October 5. After a primary campaign that revolves about his drinking problem, James Woodward defeats J. L. Key for the mayoral nomination.

November-December. Negotiations led by S.M. Inman obtain reduced rail freight rates for Atlanta businessmen.

1905 March 2. The Jewish community organizes the Standard Club.

May 13. A new Terminal Station, designed by P.T. Marye, opens.

June 28. Mrs. Isaacs Boyd creates the Atlanta Art Association.

July 11-13. Atlanta University Professor W.E.B. Du Bois chairs a Buffalo, New York meeting that founds the Niagara movement, predecessor of the N.A.A.C.P.

Alonzo Herndon organizes the Atlanta Life Insurance Company. It is today the largest private black enterprise in America, with assets of $85,000,000.

Fall. John Heisman begins fifteen years as coach of Georgia Tech's football team.

October 20. President Theodore Roosevelt visits Atlanta.

December. Since 1900 the value of Atlanta's manufacturers has risen 75 per cent. The city also boasts more home owners than any other city in the South. However, the U.S. census reports that Atlanta has the sixth highest death rate in America.

1906 February 3. The Candler Building opens, although its official dedication takes place in December.

April 25. F. L. Seeley begins to publish the Atlanta Georgian, which campaigns against convict and child labor, and for prohibition.

April-May. Reverend Thomas Sherman's plan of following his father's route through Georgia becomes a cause celebre.

Mayor Woodward's veto of higher license fees for liquor sales is overridden by the council. His continued feud with Councilman Key results in his public apology, when the mayor cannot prove charges of corruption.

September 22-25. The Atlanta Race Riot occurs, less than a month after Hoke Smith won the gubernatorial nomination on a platform of black disenfranchisement. Over 5,000 whites, infuriated by a series of alleged attacks on white women, ravage "Rusty Row," near Five Points. They attack and kill black street car passengers. Twelve people die, ten black and two white, and seventy are injured, sixty black and ten white.

December. The chamber of commerce issues a report on the riot which blames the violence on whites.

1907

January. Mayor William Joyner is inaugurated. He condemns police inefficiency and promises traffic and street improvements. Aided by the chamber of commerce, he begins a campaign to expand the city limits and to supply running water to the third of Atlanta that still lacks it.

February 7. The Atlanta Auditorium-Armory Company is organized to build a convention center.

May 25. An equestrian statue of General John B. Gordon is unveiled on the capitol grounds.

June 29. Hoke Smith is inaugurated as Georgia's governor.

October-November. During the financial panic the Neal Bank fails, but a conference of fifty leading businessmen prevents a run on Atlanta's banks.

1908

January 1. Prohibition returns to Atlanta, a statewide referendum having forced it on the traditionally "wet" city.

March. Atlanta saloons win the right to sell "near beer."

May 8. Fire in the Terminal District causes $1,000,000 in damages.

June 25. The Druid Hills Corporation is chartered and begins to build exclusive homes for Atlanta's elite.

July 3. Joel C. Harris dies at "Wren's Nest." His home will be dedicated a state monument on January 18, 1913.

September 24. James Woodward again wins the mayoral nomination in the primary.

November. Woodward is discovered drunk in the red light district.

December 1. Atlanta rejects Woodward, and elects Robert Maddox mayor.

1909

January 1. A ninth ward (Edgewood) is added to the city.

January 15. Mayor Maddox presides at a dinner honoring President-elect William Howard Taft, the first event in the new municipal auditorium. The Musical Festival Association is organized to plan concerts and raise the cultural level of Atlanta.

February 22. Dedication ceremonies open a seven story Masonic temple.

May. The First Atlanta Music Festival is held. Soprano Geraldine Ferrar sings and suggests that the city invite the Metropolitan Opera of New York to perform in Atlanta.

Summer. Atlanta opens a playground system.

September 13. Oglethorpe University is re-established, and after Atlanta donates a 137 acre site and a $250,000 endowment, it reopens in 1916.

September. The Atlanta "Crackers" win the southern league pennant, repeating their success of 1907.

November 9. The Atlanta Association of Baptist Churches is organized.

1910

January 1. The Tenth Ward (Oakland City) officially becomes

part of Atlanta, raising the city area to 12.7 square miles.

February 6. A $3,000,000 bond issue is approved, 8,475 to 66.

April 6. The Wesley Memorial Church is opened to the public.

May. The New York Metropolitan Opera Company gives four performances in Atlanta.

October 10. Cortland Winn carries every ward and easily defeats J.G. Woodward in the mayoral primary.

December. Atlanta's population of 154,839 includes 51,902 blacks (33.5 per cent).

1911

January 11. Winn is sworn in. He soon proposes that a new charter replace "a municipal maze of bewilderment."

March 8-10. The Southern Commercial Conference meets in Atlanta.

August 11. James Beavers becomes Atlanta's chief of police.

October 10. Allen Newman's peace memorial is unveiled in Piedmont Park as the city hosts the National Peace Association Jubilee.

October 11. The Debutante Club holds its first annual ball.

December 17. The new Capital City Club opens.

December. Reports show that half of Atlanta's white school children and almost 75 per cent of its blacks suffer from some physical deficiency (malnutrition, anemia, glandular disease).

1912

January 1. The Georgia Railway and Electric Company is leased to the Georgia Power Company. Mayor Winn convinces the traction combine to repave all streets where it operates a double track system.

January 31. The Sunday American is published for the first time.

Summer. The failure of the Vice-Commission to accomplish any improvement leads to a privately funded campaign that succeeds in closing may brothels; John Eagan and Police Chief Beavers share credit for the reform. Atlanta also begins to physically restore its neighborhoods. A new sewage disposal system using Imhoff tanks is put into operation, a smoke abatement program is enacted, and 35,000 citizens pledge to clean up their property.

October 15. James Woodward promises to isolate red-light activities and wins the runoff primary.

December. The chamber of commerce is told that the health department is poorly administered; "...all cases of infection, smallpox possibly excepted, among colored people are allowed to spread." The chamber demands a TB register and city milk inspection.

1913   January 2. Outgoing Mayor Winn and new incumbent Woodward join in a demand for charter revision. Before year's end, a progressive charter will decentralize city services and allow citizens the privileges of initiative, referendum and recall.

March 4. Former Atlanta lawyer Woodrow Wilson becomes president of the United States.

April 26. Mary Phagan is murdered in the National Pencil Factory. This vicious crime ultimately causes a major outbreak of Southern anti-semitism, and led to the conviction and mob murder of an innocent man, Leo Frank. Frank.

August 1. The Atlanta Rotary Club receives a charter.

September. The first class enters Atlanta Medical College, created after Atlanta Physicians and Surgeons College merged with the Atlanta School of Medicine.

September 23. The first unit of the Tallulah Falls power project goes into operation.

October 1. The Hurt Building, seventeenth largest in the world when completed, partially opens. The Healy Building on Forsyth Street is also opened this year.

October 30. The Winecoff Hotel opens.

November 3. An interurban line to Stone Mountain begins operations.

December. Atlanta's cost of living is reported to be second highest in the nation.

1914

April. The Great Imperial Session of Masonry is held in Atlanta.

May 10-12. A Shriner's convention doubles city population.

July 16. Asa Candler donates one million dollars to help reopen Emory University.

August. The First World War begins. One of its side effects is to depress the cotton industry and undermine Atlanta's economy for two years.

November 16. The Federal Reserve Bank for the Sixth District opens in the Hurt Building.

1915

January 4. Mayor Woodward takes office for his fourth term.

January 12. S.M. Inman, "First Citizen of Atlanta," dies.

January 25. A university charter is granted to Emory. Atlanta Medical College agrees to become Emory's medical school when the school reopens.

June. The Atlanta Presidents Club, whose members are presidents of civic organizations, is formed by Frederick Paxon and Earl Cone.

June 21. Governor John Slaton commutes to life imprisonment the death sentence imposed on Leo Frank. Mob violence, reacting to editorials in Tom Watson's *Jeffersonian*, forces proclamation of martial law (June 22), and troops protect Slaton until his term expires on June 26.

August 3. Chief Beavers resigns rather than be demoted for official incompetence.

August 16. Vigilantes take Leo Frank from the Milledgeville

Prison and lynch him at Marietta.

August 20. The Atlanta Council makes it unlawful to purchase a picture of Frank's lynched body.

September 1. The Scottish Rite Masons open a hospital for crippled children.

Carter Woodson establishes the Association for the Study of Negro Life and History. The Journal of Negro History first appears in 1916.

November. The Klan is reorganized atop Stone Mountain.

December. The Birth of a Nation opens in Atlanta.

A GENERATION OF CHALLENGE

1916

May 20. An area of Stone Mountain is dedicated as the site for a carved memorial to the Confederacy.

June. The first motor vehicles are purchased by the fire department.

August 24. Atlanta, a city with deficient schools, rutted streets, large debts and poor leadership, holds a mayoral primary. The chamber of commerce proposes a sixty-two year old millionaire as a reform candidate, and Coca-Cola magnate Asa Candler obtains the nomination.

September. Both Emory and Oglethorpe universities reopen for classes.

September 25. The L.Q.C. Lamar Law School opens as part of Emory University.

September 30-October 16. A street car strike against the Georgia Railway and Power Company is marked by violence until the strikers obtain higher wages, but not union recognition.

October. The Atlanta Junior League is organized.

December 6. Candler defeats Arthur Corrie and becomes mayor.

1917

January 7. General Leonard Wood visits Atlanta and chooses a site for a military training center.

March 23. Former President Taft addresses the League to Enforce Peace.

April. Caruso sings at Atlanta's last pre-war opera season.

May 21. Atlanta's "Great Fire" levels almost 300 acres and makes 10,000 citizens homeless. Over 1,000 men from Fort McPherson help fight the blaze.

June 5. Draft registration is held, and 19,214 men register; 7,890 Atlantans serve in the armed forces.

August 17. A new telephone exchange opens.

September. The first trainees enter Camp Gordon, where some 230,000 men will be trained for wartime service.

November 1. Henry Mikell is consecrated Episcopal bishop of Atlanta.

November 9. James Beavers is reinstated as police chief after charges against him are dropped due to the support of James L. Key.

November. Billy Sunday preaches an Atlanta revival.

December. Mayor Candler announces that Atlanta is virtually debt free.

Georgia Tech's undefeated "Engineers" are national collegiate football champions.

1918

February 1. Former President Taft tours Camp Gordon.

May. Air mail service between New York and Atlanta is begun, but is discontinued as unprofitable.

July 10. James L. Key wins a four man mayoral primary. Atlanta's blacks vote en masse and defeat a school bond issue to protest their dilapidated facilities. Only the promise of a new high school, to be named after David T. Howard, wins their support at a second referendum.

CHRONOLOGY

1919
January. Mayor Key attacks the Georgia Railway and Power monopoly; he suggests municipally-owned systems and total reorganization of city services.

February. The Ninth Peace Congress is held in Atlanta with Taft presiding.

April 23. Atlanta approves a bond issue of $1,000,000 for municipal improvements.

May. Atlanta approves woman suffrage, and 4,000 women vote in the September primary.

August 19. The legislature approves an eleventh ward for Atlanta.

September 5. Coca-Cola obtains a Delaware charter after Asa Candler sells the company for $25,000,000 to a group led by Ernest Woodruff and Samuel Dobbs.

November. The Women Voters League is established.

November 23. A hoax call, during a speech by Vice President Thomas Marshall, reports the death of Woodrow Wilson.

Marian Anderson receives her first concert fee, fifty dollars, for singing at Atlanta University.

1920
January 16. National Prohibition becomes law, but Atlanta pays it little heed.

April. Geraldine Ferrar shocks Atlanta by doing a strip during the opera *Zaza*.

August. Atlanta defeats the last attempt to relocate the state capital.

October 12. Key names the first legal city planning commission, a six man board headed by Howard Cutter.

December. The 2,700-seat Howard Theatre, second only to New York's Capitol Theatre, opens. It becomes Atlanta's showplace when DeGive's Opera House is razed in 1921.

Atlanta's population is 200,616, of which 31.3 per cent (62,796) is black. New territorial annexations raise the city area to 30.7 square miles by 1922.

1921 January. James Key is inaugurated for his second term.

Atlanta's first golf course, named after Mayor Key, opens to the white public.

The Citizens Trust Co. Bank (black) is organized.

July. The voters approve a bond issue of $8,850,000.

August 5. The Atlanta Girl Scout Movement is chartered.

October 1. A fireproof Cyclorama Building, to house *The Battle of Atlanta*, is dedicated.

October 27. President Harding visits Atlanta.

1922 March 15. Radio station WSB, "The Voice of the South" owned by the Atlanta *Journal*, begins to broadcast.

March 17. WGST, the *Constitution's* station, begins operations.

April 10. Atlanta adopts its first zoning ordinance. Raymond Torras becomes chief engineer of the city planning commission, a job he holds until 1948.

July 15. Atlanta opens its first swimming pool for blacks.

September. In a campaign whose leading issue is police corruption, Walter Sims wins the mayoral nomination over Chief Beavers.

December. The Wesley Memorial Hospital opens on the campus of Emory University.

1923 January. Walter Sims becomes mayor and faces a $300,000 municipal deficit. The boards of police, health, parks, and waterworks are abolished, and are replaced with councilmanic committees.

Atlanta's business community organizes the Greater Atlanta Community Chest. In other commercial news,

CHRONOLOGY 51

Robert Woodruff becomes president of Coca-Cola, while M. A. Ferst founds the Scripto Pen Company.

December 12. Chief Beavers is suspended by the council at the demand of Mayor Sims.

December 20. The $1,000,000 Spring Street Viaduct is opened to traffic.

1924 January 19. Gutzon Borglum's head of General Robert E. Lee, cut into the granite of Stone Mountain, is unveiled. His achievement is later blasted away when a new designer, Augustus Lukeman, takes over the project.

April 19. The $6,000,000 Biltmore Hotel opens.

Rich's Department Store opens a new main building at Broad and Alabama streets.

May 1. Atlanta's new municipal market opens.

May 24. Druid Hills Golf Club burns down.

June. Spelman Seminary becomes a college.

September 24. Mayor Sims defeats James Key in the primary. Among the new aldermen is a young man named William Hartsfield who campaigns for airport development.

1925 January. Sims is again inaugurated; he presides over a city with one of the lowest property tax rates in America, only $1.05 per $100.

Fifty Methodist congregations form Goodwill Industries.

October 5. "Forward Atlanta," a chamber of commerce project to boost the city, begins operations. In the next five years over 760 businesses valued at $35,000,000 relocate in Atlanta.

Candler Field is leased to serve as a Municipal airport.

1926 January 9. Joel Hurt, "Atlanta's Master Builder", dies.

January. Sears Roebuck opens it first store in Atlanta.

February-March. A new house numbering system is installed.

May 8. Atlanta accepts Mrs. Joseph Madison High's offer of her home, on condition it be converted into an art museum; the museum opens in October.

May 29. Bath houses open in Piedmont Park.

July 26. The Pullman Company opens a plant in Atlanta.

September 15. Regular air mail service to Miami begins.

September 22. Isaac N. Ragsdale defeats four opponents for the mayoral nomination. He will oversee expenditure of an $8,000,000 bond issue approved by the voters.

Runway grading for an expanded city airport begins.

1927

January 3. Ragsdale is inaugurated; he pledges to complete the city viaduct system and run an economical administration. He will be forced to accept the triumphant return to power of Police Chief Beavers.

February 25. The Georgia Power Company is reincorporated.

March 21. The R.H. Macy Company opens its first department store in the South.

July 27. A new Atlanta planning commission is approved.

The locomotive Texas, hero of the "Andrews Raid" of 1862, goes on display at the Cyclorama Building.

October 11. Atlanta celebrates "Lindbergh Day."

1928

January 1. The suburb of East Lake (population 2,000) is annexed.

April. A Chevrolet plant beings to operate; a Fisher Body plant is added in June.

June 29. Morris Rich dies.

August 5. The Atlanta World, a black weekly, is founded

by William A. Scott.

October 28. Egleston Memorial Children's Hospital opens.

December. Undefeated Georgia Tech, victor over Notre Dame, is declared national champion and goes on to win the Rose Bowl.

1929

January. Ragsdale begins his second term as mayor.

January 15. Martin Luther King Jr. is born in Atlanta.

March. The Central Avenue and Pryor Street viaducts open. Also opened to traffic this year is the Mitchell Street Bridge.

March 12. Asa Candler dies.

April 1. The Atlanta university system of largely black schools is organized. Atlanta University, Morehouse and Spelman Colleges, and the Atlanta School of Social Work agree to share their facilities. Clark College, Morris Brown College, and Gammon Theological Seminary will soon join this cooperative venture, which is today the largest center for black education in the nation.

April 13. Atlanta purchases Candler Field for its municipal airport.

The twenty-one story Rhodes-Haverty Building is completed; its unusual tall tower design is by Francis P. Smith.

July 27. A four year term for Atlanta's mayor wins legislative approval. Later in the session, a thirteenth ward is added to the city.

Dorothy Alexander organizes a group that becomes the Atlanta Ballet Company.

Ralph McGill joins the Constitution as a sportswriter.

November 20. The First National Bank of Georgia is created as the result of three mergers.

December. Atlanta retail sales reach their highest level, $180,600,000; a decade later they will be only $172,300,000.

Indicative of city growth is a survey by <u>The American City</u>, which reports a total of thirty-one Atlanta skyscrapers.

1930

January 1. A Greater Atlanta of 179 square miles is created as five suburbs are annexed. Its population of 270,366 (90,075 blacks) makes Atlanta the second city of the South and 22nd in the nation.

January 30. The Atlanta Gas Light Company begins to supply natural gas to the city.

February 22. The fourteen story semi-Gothic city hall, constructed at a cost of $1,000,000, officially opens. Designed by G. Lloyd Preacher, it contrasts nicely with the nearby capitol.

April 18. The new Union Station opens.

June 18. Mayor Ragsdale's administration has suffered fifteen graft indictments in 1929. James Key wins the mayoral primary with a campaign against civic corruption and takes office January 1, 1931.

September 29. Atlanta honors Bobby Jones, who has completed golf's "grand slam"-- the U.S. Open and Amateur, and the British Open and Amateur titles.

1931

May. The Atlanta <u>Constitution</u> wins the Pulitzer Prize for exposing municipal corruption.

The nation's first passenger terminal opens at Atlanta Airport.

October 16-18. The Hebrew Benevolent Temple is dedicated.

Mayor Key battles "drys" who prevented him from teaching Sunday school classes because he claimed "prohibition is abominable." Key is ultimately expelled from membership in Grace Methodist Church.

1932

Its merger with Milton and Campbell counties triples the size of Fulton County.

March. The <u>Atlanta World</u> becomes a daily newspaper.

April. James Beavers retires after a long and stormy career in law enforcement.

July. Thousands demonstrate against inadaquate city relief measures.

August. The Atlanta Negro Chamber of Commerce is organized.

October 24. Franklin D. Roosevelt speaks at an Atlanta rally.

1933

January 13. The city council cuts city salaries by 20 per cent. Rich's Department Store, largest in Atlanta, soon announces a policy of accepting city scrip from municipal employees and giving change in U.S. currency.

May 19. Bars in Atlanta legally sell 3.2 per cent beer for the first time since 1916.

July 6. First National Bank President John Ottley is kidnapped, then freed after payment of a $40,000 ransom.

October 4. Some 50,000 Atlantans march to honor the N.R.A.'s "Blue Eagle."

October 5. Sleeping berth air service to New York City is instituted.

December 2. A $3,000,000 post office opens on Forsyth Street.

1934

August. Atlanta Junior College opens.

September. Labor unions shut down all but one of Atlanta's textile mills and provoke two weeks of intermittent violence; only martial law ultimately restores peace.

September 26. J.L. Key wins the mayoral primary over Roy LeGraw. He pledges continued support for F.D.R. and the New Deal.

1935

March 14. Atlanta's ward system is changed by the legislature. Thirteen wards are reduced to six, and the thirty-nine member council is cut to eighteen members as of January 1, 1937.

September 18. A sewer bond issue of $1,175,000 is approved by the voters.

November 29. President Roosevelt dedicates the first public housing project in America, Techwood Homes. It is the first of eight Atlanta projects constructed before 1941.

December 28, 1935 - January 2, 1936. Atlanta is ice bound after a storm causes $2,000,000 in damages.

1936

April. The First Dogwood Festival is held.

June 28. Margaret Mitchell's <u>Gone With the Wind</u> goes on sale in Atlanta. In America it sells half a million copies in the months -- and total sales now stand at 21,000,000 copies.

The <u>Battle of Atlanta</u> Cyclorama is turned into a three dimensional display with funds provided through the W.P.A.

September. Techwood Homes, 604 units, is occupied.

September 12. Tom Finch, a black orderly at Grady Hospital, is shot five times by the mob that "arrested" him for an alleged crime.

September 23. William Hartsfield (12,348), candidate of the Atlanta business elite, defeats James Key (8,174) in the mayoral primary.

November. A three-month strike begins at the Fisher Body Plant.

November 14. Clark Howell, an editor of the <u>Constitution</u> since 1889, dies.

December 23. The body of Mack Henry Brown is discovered. His murder is attributed to his familiarity with a white woman.

THE HARTSFIELD ERA

1937

January. Hartsfield inaugural address attacks police corruption and promises reduction in city debt. He advocates aviations improvement and development of the Chattahoochee River.

CHRONOLOGY

April. Atlanta is designated a Roman Catholic bishopric.

University Homes, a 675 unit P.W.A. project, is completed.

May. Margaret Mitchell wins the Pulitzer Prize for Gone With the Wind.

August 1. The Journal opens its second radio station, WAGA.

August 8. The Citizens Fact Finding Movement of Georgia is organized to work for reform.

August. The roof of the Municipal Auditorium collapses.

1938

February 5. Thomas Harrison Reed presents a report on county/city consolidation to a meeting of civic leaders.

March 23. Maynard Jackson, who will be elected Atlanta's first black mayor in 1974, is born in Dallas.

March 30. Fulton County votes to allow liquor sales, and they begin on April 25.

May 16. Fire at the Terminal Hotel kills thirty-five persons.

June 11. The Atlanta Housing Authority is appointed; Charles Palmer is its first chairman.

Summer. Atlanta continues to grow. A reconstructed auditorium opens, and the nation's first air traffic control tower goes into operation at Atlanta Airport.

November. Tobacco Road begins a seven year run at the Erlanger Theatre.

1939

January 18. The Catholic Co-Cathedral of Christ the King is dedicated.

Charter amendments give more power to the mayor's office. Hartsfield forces the council to accept a Model Budget Law, wherein only 99 per cent of a previous year's revenues may be allocated. Atlanta adopts one of Thomas Reed's recommendations and becomes the first large city in the South to enact a civil service law.

July 1. Charles Palmer reports that 54.85 per cent of all Atlanta's housing is sub-standard.

July. The World Baptist Congress meets in Atlanta.

December 15. David Selznick's Gone With the Wind has its world premier at the Loew's Grand Theatre in Atlanta. The film, which cost $4,250,000 to produce, wins ten Academy Awards and over the years has grossed well over $130,000,000.

December 17. Hearst's Georgia-American ceases publication

1940

January 30. A ten-inch snowfall cripples the city.

March 7. Ike Gaston, a white man who abused his wife, dies after being whipped by the Klan.

May. The Metropolitan Opera returns to Atlanta for the first time since 1930.

July 3. The council approves a $4,000,000 bond issue for schools and hospitals.

July 22. The new national headquarters of Coca-Cola opens.

September 4. Roy LeGraw defeats Hartsfield by 111 votes and wins the mayoral nomination.

September. The John Hope Homes, which replaced 500 slum dwellings with 606 apartments, receives its first tenants.

October 10. Work begins on the Atlanta Naval Air Station.

November 11. The Auditorium is severely damaged by fire.

November 23. Joel Hurt Park is opened to the public.

December. Atlanta's city population reaches 302,288, with over a third of the total (104,533) being blacks. Although Atlanta is the heart of a metropolitan region of almost 600,000, city growth has slowed appreciably during the thirties to only 11.8 per cent. From 1940-50 population rises only 9.6 per cent.

CHRONOLOGY

1941   May. A new farmer's market opens and handles $6,000,000 in business by years end, a figure that rises to $10,000,000 in 1942 and $42,000,000 by 1952.

Atlanta conpletes four New Deal housing projects, the Grady, Eagan, Herndon and Capitol Houses.

1942   February 29. A B-29 assembly plant is announced for Marietta.

Atlanta Airport installs America's first instrument approach system.

May 27. Hartsfield defeats seven oponents in a special primary, and wins the right to replace Roy LeGraw, who has been called to active duty.

November 12-13. The anti-air craft cruiser _Atlanta_ is sunk off Guadalcanal.

December. William Alexander, coach at Georgia Tech from 1920-1945, is named "Coach of the Year."

1943   March. The reconstructed Auditorium opens.

April 30. The Georgia W.P.A. ceases operations.

September. The Bell B-29 Plant (later Lockheed Aviation) goes into operation.

December 10. Thornwell Jacobs resigns as president of Oglethorpe University.

1944   January 20. Explosions and fire at the Atlanta Ordinance Depot destroy $2,000,000 worth of supplies.

March. A group of prisoners at the Atlanta Penitentiary volunteer to test experimental malarial drugs.

June 5. Ernest Woodruff of Coco-Cola dies.

December 3. The cruiser _Atlanta_, authorized only after a campaign led by Margaret Mitchell, is commissioned.

December 6. A mutiny of prisoners at the penitentiary is mediated by Atlanta _Journal_ columnist Morgan Blank.

1945	April 13. Atlanta mourns President Roosevelt as his funeral cortege passes through the city.
	September 9. Hartsfield again wins the mayoral primary.
	October 1. The Fulton-Dekalb Hospital Authority is created to administer all area hospitals after January 1, 1946.
	October 18. A memorial to Father O'Reilly, hero of the fire of 1864, is unveiled at city hall.
1946	April. The first Atlanta Book Fair is held.
	May 9. The AFL-CIO demands that Georgia investigate the Klan after a massive cross-burning ceremony on Stone Mountain.
	August 14. Atlanta and Fulton County citizens approve bond issues of over $40,000,000 to finance new school construction and implement an express highway plan developed by H. W. Lockner and Company.
	December 7. The Winecoff Hotel, lacking both fire escapes and sprinklers, is swept by fire, and 119 persons die; another one hundred are injured.
	December 21. Governor-elect Eugene Tallmadge dies, and Georgia will experience the "Year of the Three Governors" in 1947.
1947	January. The Atlanta Symphony Orchestra is created.
	February. Herbert Jenkins becomes chief of police and acts to reduce the power of the KKK-dominated police union.
	March 18. A black <u>Daily World</u> reporter is granted a press card by Congress.
	March 27. The Metropolitan Planning Commission is established.
	May. The Metropolitan Opera returns to Atlanta for a week's engagement.
	George Goodwin of the <u>Journal</u> wins a Pulitzer Prize for

disclosing vote frauds.

Summer. Atlanta sponsors free pop concerts, and places historic markers on twenty-three downtown sites.

August. Voters in Buckhead and Cascade Heights defeat Hartsfield's annexation proposals.

September. The School of Social Work becomes part of Atlanta University; the University of Georgia opens an Atlanta Division.

October. Delta Airlines opens a $1,000,000 headquarters in Atlanta.

December 1. Atlanta authorizes black policemen "under conditions as will not create any strife or tension between the races." The police union wins a stay order on December 15 to prevent appointment of black policemen.

December. A Ford assembly plant opens in Hopeville. Atlanta enjoys a postwar boom which creates about 25,000 new jobs.

1948

February 26. Eight black policemen are added to the Atlanta police department, as the stay order is overturned.

March 29. Another Rich's department store opens for business.

May 9. A new passenger terminal opens at Atlanta Municipal Airport.

June 16. A General Motors plant opens at Doraville.

September 8. The Rich Foundation donates WABE-FM to the Atlanta Public School System.

September 29. The South's first TV station, WSB-TV, begins operations.

December 19. The Atlanta Urban League denounces separate school systems for the two races. Blacks live primarily in the seventh section of Atlanta that is slums, an area with 40 per cent of the city's population. Those sections contain 72 per cent of Atlanta's juvenile delinquency, 60 per cent of its crime, and 69 per cent of its TB.

1949 April 11. Atlanta's last non-electric trolley makes its final run.

May 1-20. Transit workers strike for wages, pensions, and better working conditions.

May 2. In a move against the KKK, the council bans the wearing of masks except at festivals.

August 11. Margaret Mitchell is run down by a car and dies of her injuries on August 16.

September 7. After the Supreme Court of the U.S. declares the all-white primary to be unconstitutional (1947), Atlanta's blacks participate for the first time in choosing a mayor. Hartsfield wins bi-racial support for his scheme to expand Atlanta's boundaries and is easily renominated.

October 3. Radio Station WERD, owned and operated by blacks, begins operations.

1950 January. The Plan of Improvement for the Governments of Atlanta and Fulton County is adopted; it enacts many of the Reed proposals of 1938 and becomes the blueprint for Atlanta's revival.

March 6. Federal Judge M. Neil Andrews rules that films are subject to local censorship and the city can ban Lost Boundaries, a movie about "passing." Also in March, the federal courts sentence Fulton County officials to a year in jail and fines for turning black prisoners over to a White mob which beat them.

March 18. The merger of the Journal with the Constitution is announced.

April 16. Edward Harkness Hall is dedicated as the Administration Building of Atlanta University.

June 24. A thirty-seven day transit strike ends when the Georgia Power Company sells its transit facilities to the Atlanta Transit Company.

June 28. Fulton County and Atlanta approve the creation of eight consolidated programs.

September. Petitions by blacks against a segregated school system are denied.

October. The U.S. Supreme Court refuses to review a charge of discriminatory wage scales for Atlanta's black teachers.

December. Atlanta's population is 437,785 while its Metropolitan District has a population of 726,989.

1951

January. The first copy of the Atlanta Economic Review is published by the University of Georgia.

February 16. The Atlanta Journal and Constitution win a struggle against Governor Herman Tallmadge as the legislature adjourns without restricting their right to publish.

April. The Peachtree Hotel opens on the site where the Winecoff Hotel burned down.

1952

January 1. Annexation of eighty-two square miles is completed.

June 22. The Hughes Spalding Pavilion is dedicated at Grady Hospital.

October 14. The Daily World, still the only black daily in America, endorses Dwight Eisenhower for president; both the Journal and the Constitution back Adlai Stevenson.

November 9. The Ernest Woodruff Medical Research Building opens at Emory University.

1953

April 12. Abby Rockefeller Hall opens on the campus of Spelman College.

The Theatre of the Stars holds its first series of Broadway entertainments.

October 5. A new charter and code of general ordinances is approved. At the same time, a coalition of blacks and middle class whites once again return Hartsfield to the mayoralty.

Atlanta's first postwar housing project, the 990-unit Carver Community, opens. Almost unnoticed is a new architectural firm opened by John Portman, the man who will practically rebuild downtown Atlanta in the 1960's.

1954 The Fulton National Bank Building, first post-war skyscraper, opens.

December 22. A new zoning plan is adopted for the Atlanta Metropolitan Area.

1955 February. Louis Lautier of the Daily World is the first black elected to the National Press Club.

April 5. Memorial services are held in the Sisters Chapel, Spelman College, honoring Trevor Arnett, crusader for better education for blacks.

July-August. A long battle over school integration begins when Horace Ward tries to enter law school. On August 1, Georgia orders all black teachers to quit the NAACP or lose their teaching licenses, an order rescinded on August 5.

November 7. The U.S. Supreme Court bars segregation on Atlanta's municipal golf courses.

December 24. Atlanta's golf courses are integrated without incident.

1957 January 9. Black ministers briefly integrate Atlanta's buses.

John Portman and Ben Massell present the idea for Peachtree Center to Atlanta.

September. Hartsfield defeats Fulton County Commissioner Archie Lindsey in the primary. The voters also approve another bond issue.

October. Hartsfield crushes the petition campaign of Lester Maddox, and is elected mayor once more. Fortune magazine lists him among the top nine mayors in America, and also ranks Atlanta first in regional planning and noise abatement success.

1958 August. Sixty Georgians from Dahlonega present the state with enough panned gold to gild the Capitol dome.

October 12. A Reformed Jewish temple on Peachtree Road is bombed, and five members fo the National States Rights Party are indicted for the act on October 17. Ralph McGill's editorials on the crime win him a Pulitzer Prize (1959).

November 14. Hartsfield declares that Atlantans must choose whether or not their school system can be closed by the state in order to prevent integration.

December 31. Atlanta's retail sales have increased 600 per cent since 1939; the city now makes 12.8 per cent of all wholesale sales in the South. It remains politically weak in Georgia, however, where it pays 20 per cent of all taxes and obtains only 5 per cent of total state aid.

1959

January 9. Atlanta's segregated bus system is declared unconstitutional by a federal court. Atlanta's black ministers counsel their congregations not to test the decision immediately.

January 10. Georgia's colleges are ordered not to bar applicants on the basis of race.

May 19. The Atlanta Public Library integrates when Mrs. Maynard Jackson receives a library card.

May 22. The library announces that The Rabbit's Wedding, a story for three to seven year olds about the marriage of a black rabbit to a white rabbit, has been removed from the open shelves.

The total integration of the Atlanta Police Department is finally achieved by Chief Jenkins.

1960

January 11. Georgia Governor Vandiver threatens to withhold all state money from integrated schools.

May 17. Violent confrontation between blacks and whites is avoided only by good police work and by the willingness of Lonnie King to lead his Atlanta University marchers away from the state capital grounds.

June 1. Ralph McGill is named publisher of the Constitution as Eugene Patterson becomes editor. The Constitution is ranked eighth in the nation in "news coverage, integrity and public service." In the black community, the Atlanta Inquirer is founded to combat the conservatism of the Daily World; among its editors is a young man named Julian Bond.

November. Martin Luther King and seventy-five students are arrested for "sitting in" at Rich's department store, where blacks may buy but not try on clothes, eat lunch, or go to the bathroom.

December. Ivan Allan Jr. is named president of the chamber of commerce, and the businessmen unamimously endorse his Six Point Program for Atlanta development. Atlanta's population has grown to 487,455 and the metropolitan area population has passed the million mark.

1961

February 15. One white and seven black ministers are arrested for supporting the "jail in" of the students arrested at Rich's.

March 7. The chamber of commerce announces a plan to desegregate Atlanta lunchrooms. In return, a black boycott of Atlanta stores is to end.

May. The chamber of commerce begins to publish a monthly magazine called Atlanta. It also announces a new Forward Atlanta effort to develop the "national potential" of the city. Indicative of Atlanta's growing stature is the opening of John Portman and H. Griffith Edwards' Merchandise Mart, and the completion of a $20,000,000 jet air terminal.

August 30. Nine blacks integrate four Atlanta high schools.

September 4. Atlanta police disperse a rally of 250 segregationists.

September 18. Three black students integrate Georgia Tech.

September 22. Ivan Allen Jr. wins the mayoral runoff primary when he defeats Lester Maddox.

September 28. As 177 Atlanta restaurants peacefully desegregate, the Hartsfield era comes to an end.

METROPOLIS OF THE SOUTH

1962

January. Allen is inaugurated for his first four year term. He soon personally helps integrate city hall's cafeteria, and grants a municipal work week of forty hours.

March 29. Paul Hallinan is installed as Roman Catholic archbishop of Atlanta.

June 3. A charter plane crash at Orly Airport outside Paris kills 106 Atlanta patrons of music and art.

June 10. Archbishop Hallinan announces the desegregation of eighteen elementary and five high schools run by the Atlanta Diocese.

September. The county unit system of representation is declared unconstitutional. As a result, the representation of Atlanta in the state senate rises from one to twelve in 1963; among the new senators will be one Republican and one black.

November 10. The Atlanta postmaster is suspended for non-compliance with President John Kennedy's anti-discrimination policy.

1963

May. A $39,000,000 bond issue is approved only one year after an $80,000,000 proposal was defeated; among its provisions is $9,000,000 for a new opera house.

June 6. Mayor Allen's Atlanta-Fulton County Stadium Authority meets for the first time.

July 25. Mayor Allen announces his support for the Civil Rights Bill pending in Congress.

July 26. At the request of President Kennedy, Mayor Allen testifies on behalf of the Civil Rights Bill; the mayor's stand is not supported by the Constitution.

1964

April 15. Ground breaking ceremonies are held for Atlanta Stadium.

June 12. The first issue of the Atlanta Times, a newspaper that lasts only until August 31, 1965, appears.

July 22. The federal court upholds the Civil Rights Act provision that bars discrimination in public accomodations. Among those ordered to integrate is the Pickrick Restaurant, where Lester Maddox used a gun to expel blacks on July 3.

Rather than comply with the court's order, Maddox closes his restaurant in August.

The J. W. E. Bowen Housing Project opens as does the "pagoda" of the Fulton Federal Savings and Loan Association.

October 14. President William Bartholomay of the Milwaukee Braves signs a twenty-five year lease to use Atlanta Stadium for his baseball team.

December. Atlanta's Community Improvement Program is formed to improve neighborhoods and community services.

1965

January 27. Atlanta honors Martin Luther King, Nobel Peace Prize winner (1964).

April. A day care center opens at the Bowen Houses. Atlanta's fifteen projects house 30,444 citizens in 8,874 units, and sixteen additional projects are planned.

April 9-11. A three game series between the Braves and the Detroit Tigers helps dedicate Atlanta Stadium. The Braves, however, play their 1965 season in Milwaukee.

June 6. Over five hundred Klan members march in Atlanta.

Summer. Atlanta avoids a "long, hot summer" when Mayor Allen gets businessmen to donate seven swimming pools for use in the black areas of Atlanta.

June 23. Mayor Allen names a commission on crime and juvenile delinquency led by Griffin B. Bell. One commission finding ranks Atlanta as world leader in consumption of non-tax paid whiskey.

September 13. Atlanta receives a $6,300,000 poverty grant from Congress.

October. Mayor Allen soundly defeats Muggsy Smith, 53,233 to 21,907 to win another term.

December. Atlanta's employment has increased 38 per cent since Allen took office, and its unemployment rate of 2.2 per cent is the lowest in the nation.

1966

Chief Jenkins orders "nigger" and "boy" dropped from the

police vocabulary. A crime prevention bureau is organized to ease police relations with ghetto residents.

January 10. The Georgia House refuses to seat Representative Julian Bond because of his stand against the Vietnam War.

January 28. The National League orders the Braves to ignore a Wisconsin circuit court order and to open their baseball season in Atlanta.

April 12. The first official National League baseball game is played in Atlanta Stadium.

Six Flags Over Georgia, a 276 acre amusement complex in West Atlanta, opens.

The Atlanta Historical Association purchases the Swan House (1928) as its headquarters.

June 6-9. Three quarters of Atlanta's firemen strike the city, demanding reduction of their sixty hour work week.

July 5. The National Opinion Survey shows that integration in Atlanta has not led to a decline of housing values; neither has it led to greater social integration.

September. The Atlanta Falcons bring the National Football League to Atlanta.

September 6-11. Blacks riot in the Summerhill area. Thirty-five persons are injured, 138 arrested, and Mayor Allen is toppled from a car by a mob before the disturbances cease. Stokley Carmichael of the Student Non-Violent Coordinating Committee is indicted for inciting the disturbances (September 13). During the riot, Julian Bond announces his resignation from SNCC for "personal reasons."

December 5. A unamimous Supreme Court decision upholds Julian Bond's right to be seated in the Georgia legislature.

1967

January 23. The U.S. Supreme Court rejects Milwaukee's anti-trust action against Atlanta and baseball.

May. Eugene Patterson of the Constitution wins the Pulitzer

Prize for his editorials supporting Representative Bond's right to a legislative seat.

John Portman's Regency Hyatt Hotel opens; its "Blue Bubble" is now an Atlanta landmark.

June 19-20. Racial unrest follows an address by Stokley Carmichael -- one black dies and three others are seriously wounded before Mayor Allen proclaims a curfew.

July 27. President Lyndon Johnson names Atlanta's Police Chief Herbert Jenkins a member of the Kerner "Riot Commission."

November 7. Rufus E. Clement, president of Atlanta University since 1937, dies. In 1953 he was elected to serve on the Board of Education, the first black to win a city election since Reconstruction.

Two Georgia Tech graduates, Steve Fuller and Jack Patterson, begin to plan a private development called Underground Atlanta, which opens in May, 1969.

1968

January. A neo-classical governor's mansion is dedicated to replace the James Mansion in use since the Reconstructtion. Also opened in this year are the new Equitable Insurance Building and the Trust Company of Georgia Building.

March 28. Cleveland Sellers of SNCC is convicted of draft evasion, a crime he argued was a protest against the Vietnam War.

April 6. The body of Martin Luther King, assassinated on April 4 in Memphis, is put on public view at the Ebenezer Baptist Church. President Lyndon Johnson proclaims a National Day of Mourning. On April 9, King is buried after a nationally televised funeral march through the streets of Atlanta.

June 11-12. Four convicts take twenty-five hostages after they fail to escape from the Federal Penitentiary. They free the hostages only after the *Journal* publishes a list of prisoner complaints.

September 10. Ralph Abernathy, King's successor as SCLC leader, is arrested for encouraging 800 black garbage workers to strike against Atlanta.

October. The Atlanta Hawks bring NBA Basketball to the city.

October 24-29. Two units of the $13,000,000 Memorial Arts Center are dedicated. Today the complex houses the Alliance Resident Theatre, the Symphony Orchestra, the High Museum and the Atlanta College of Art.

November 8. Maynard Jackson, a black official who announced his candidacy for the U.S. Senate only in June, carries Atlanta but is crushed in the statewide results.

1969

January. Mayor Allen announces he will not seek a third term.

January 14. The Atlanta Municipal Theatre, whose initial production was the satire Red, White and Maddox, discontinues operations but is reorganized in March.

February 4. Ralph McGill dies of a heart attack.

April. Peaceful demonstrations at the capitol mark the anniversary of Martin Luther King's death.

June 24. The Justice Department announces a suit against the West Peachtree Corporation for a discriminatory rental policy.

The Atlanta Historical Association takes possession of the Tullie Smith Home.

October 21. Sam Massell overcomes a charge of corrupt campaign financing and wins the mayoral nomination against Rodney Cook. Massell becomes the first Jewish mayor of Atlanta, and his vice mayor, Maynard Jackson, is black. Blacks on the board of aldermen increase from one to five, while three others are elected to the board of education.

December. Fifteen skyscrapers of twenty or more floors have been started since 1960 -- over $1.3 billion of construction has been completed, with another $450,000,000 underway.

1970

January 15. The Martin Luther King Memorial center is

dedicated.

March 20. Federal courts approve a geographic zoning plan that will increase integrated schools to 64.5 per cent of Atlanta's total. Massive bussing of students is ruled unacceptable.

April 22. After a strike lasting since March 17, pay raises are approved for 2,300 city employees. Mayor Massell rehires the workers he had threatened with final dismissal.

May. The Confederate Memorial on Stone Mountain is completed after fifty years of effort. Walker Hancock was consulting sculptor.

May 22. Vice President Spiro Agnew attacks the Constitution as part of the "liberal news media."

June 4. Lester Maddox pickets the Constitution to protest its opposition to cleansing America of "Communists, anarchists, and nasty people."

September 3-7. The First Congress of African People is held at Atlanta University.

November. Jimmy Carter is elected governor of Georgia on an anti-establishment platform. He will reduce Georgia's bureaucracy and achieve greater racial understanding during his term in office.

December. The "Hub of the South" ranks as America's twentieth largest city, with a population of 497,421. It is served by six railroads, nine combination airlines, five federal highways and 350 regulated motor carriers; of the 500 largest industrial firms in America, 430 have offices, plants or warehouses in Atlanta. However, the white "flight to the suburbs" has made Atlanta 51 per cent black with a school system over 65 per cent black.

1971

August-September. Ernest Medina is tried and found not guilty of the Mylai Massacre in Vietnam by a court martial held in Fort McPherson.

November. Atlanta voters approve a ten year 4 per cent sales tax; it will finance a rapid transit system (MARTA) combining fifty miles of high speed rail, fifteen miles of rapid bus ways and 1500 miles of surface transportation. The new tax goes into effect April, 1972 and MARTA soon drops fares from forty cents to fifteen cents.

December. Atlanta unemployment is only 3.6 per cent for 1971, showing job gains of 25,000 yearly since 1961.

Hartsfield International Airport ranks second in America in emplaned passengers -- and fourth in the world in total passengers.

Vice Mayor Jackson pushes housing/construction industry reforms and backs a tenant rent strike.

1972

September. Atlanta's school system has 72,129 blacks and only 21,850 whites; 106 of 153 schools are designated "segregated" as the city endorses "neighborhood" schools in an attempt to stem white flight.

November. Andrew Young is elected the South's first black congressman since Reconstruction. A school busing plan is delayed by action of a federal court.

1973

January. A freezing ice storm disrupts power to 500,000 Atlanta residents for up to six days.

March. Southern Airways announces plans to construct an $18,000,000 maintenance facility at Hartsfield Airport, a facility opened in 1976.

April 4. The federal court orders busing of 2,761 whites to integrate Atlanta schools. National NAACP condemns its local chapter's accomodation to racial isolation, even though the system is almost 80 per cent black.

Woodruff Foundation gives Atlanta a central city park.

October 16. In a campaign that heightens racial feeling, Maynard Jackson defeats Massell and becomes Atlanta's first black mayor. Wyche Fowler defeats Hosea Williams for president of the city council, largely on the basis of his opposition to more expressways. The bi-racial team will have to deal with a dwindling tax base, growing crime rates and MARTA system costs, but voter approval of a new charter strenghtens the mayor's office.

December. Atlanta has the highest gonorreah rate in America for the period June-December, 1973.

1974

January 7. Maynard Jackson is sworn in -- the "youngest, fattest, blackest" mayor in America. His council is 50 per cent black. Jackson asserts that Atlanta's major problem is crime -- there were 271 murders in 1973.

February 22. Ground breaking for the MARTA subway takes place.

April 1. After seventy-one years in Chattanooga, the Southern Newspaper Publishers Association relocates in Atlanta.

April 8. Hank Aaron hits his 715th home run and surpasses Babe Ruth's career record.

June 18. The portrait of Martin Luther King, hung in the capitol by Governor Carter, is defaced.

May-August. Mayor Jackson attempts to dismiss Police Chief John Inman. Inman argues the unconstitutional nature of the new charter (imposed by the state legislature) and maintains his post until he retires on pension. His replacement, Reginald Eaves, is named public safety commissioner.

June 21. The Atlanta school board rejects a textbook advancing the divine theory of creation as having "numerous errors in terms of established biological fact."

June 30. Mrs. Martin Luther King, Senior is murdered during services in Ebenezer Baptist Church. Mayor Jackson orders flags hung at half-mast until July 3.

July. The army's first woman chaplain, Reverend Alice Hendersen, is commissioned in Atlanta.

December. Atlanta is estimated to be 55 per cent black.

1975

January. Over two thousand unemployed people cause damage while applying for 225 Atlanta public service jobs.

February. The Georgia legislature begins to maneuver to annex white suburbs to Atlanta. Jackson gives the cause tepid support.

March 24. A tornado hits Atlanta, killing three persons and injuring fifty; it also wrecks the governor's mansion.

April 17. Jackson reappoints Eaves as public safety commissioner, although his chauffeur is an admitted felon, and despite the fact that many state and local police departments will no longer exchange intelligence with Atlanta.

The <u>Constitution</u> runs a seven-part article attacking the Jackson administration.

May 9. The first Mayor's Day for the Arts is held.

September-October. Enrollment of white pupils in Atlanta's schools drops to 13 per cent as a school strike further damages the system's credibility.

1976

February. The seventy story, 723-foot Peachtree Center Plaza Hotel, designed by John Portman, opens, as does a brand new Hilton Hotel. Atlanta ranks as America's third largest convention center.

April. Statistics show Eaves has reduced Atlanta's crime rate, increased police training, and hired and fired black officers on merit alone. The police force has grown from 952 in 1970 to 1,561 in 1975.

May. The $14,000,000 World of Syd and Marty Krofft opens.

Summer. Atlanta's restoration continues; in Inman Park, a slum in 1970, renovation of 1,000 out of 1,400 homes is under way.

July 14. Former Governor Jimmy Carter becomes the Democratic nominee for president. His organization is dominated by Atlanta-based politicians and lawyers.

November 2. Carter is elected president of the United States.

DOCUMENTS

Modern Atlanta has often been unfairly characterized as "instant city." Certainly the architects and urban planners who today flock to its downtown area document the attractions Atlanta has for the builder. Atlanta is to them living testimony of the triumph of their craft, the symbol of a New South, an "urban wilderness" that now works. But as the preceding chronology makes clear, Atlanta has fulfilled many visions throughout its history; never was it only another version of the prescribed southern or urban pattern. Atlanta's birth was due to the railroads that were ignored by the rest of the South; it was thus a regional center long before it was Georgia's capital. Unlike other southern citizens, Atlantans never had to worry about the debilitating effects of climate and disease, for they occupied the highest American urban center (1050 feet) east of Denver. Atlanta never represented the bucolic South; its image was based on its business community's acumen and iniative. Yet despite many unique qualities, Atlanta remained always southern; the city was once described as a lady whose Yankee mink covered a Confederate slip. Less kind were those commentators who described Atlanta as a city of northern overseers exploiting southern riches. Atlanta thus has played many historical parts and its newest transformation, a "shock city" leading America into the future, is only the latest role for the "Gate City."

In the documents that follow, the "Hub of the South" is discovered at various stages of its frequently stormy history. Atlanta's physical reality has changed -- railroads have bowed before the plane, the shacks of Terminus have become the skyline of a modern city -- but its optimism through the decades has remained constant. Few American cities today convey the sense of purpose and accomplishment that characterize modern Atlanta, and that unflagging spirit is certainly the force that makes its urban history so exciting.

EARLY ATLANTA - 1839

As railroads pushed into northern Georgia, where only the army and the Indians had previously reigned, a small community named Terminus (Atlanta) was created. As three lines slowly converged on this village, rough railroad men, their women, and the inevitable panoply of storekeepers, whiskey dealers, and settlers streamed into the area. John J. Thrasher, in an interview he gave to the Atlanta Constitution, August 1, 1897, described the social environment of Terminus in 1839.

Source: The Atlanta Constitution, August 1, 1897.

I was building the Monroe embankment. My foreman was a man named Mulligan. You might suspect from his name that he was Irish. He was a good workman. I got him from the State road because he had had experience in railroad work, and I needed such a man to look after my laborers. Mulligan was a married man, and so were others of my laborers, -- the most of whom lived in the neighborhood.... These shacks were rude cabins made from roughly sawed timber. All of them had dirt floors. There was not a plank floor among them all.

Mrs. Mulligan heard that the shacks were not floored with boards and she refused to move down here with her husband unless her cabin was floored with planks. She was the foreman's wife, and she felt that she was entitled to something better than a dirt floor. Mulligan would not stay with me unless his wife moved down, and so there was nothing for me to do but to buy the lumber and put a wooden floor in the Mulligan shack; and so I had to go out to Collier's Mill for the material. Well, I bought a load or two of puncheon, and laid the best floor I could for Mrs. Mulligan. Her husband thought it would please her, and she came down.

No sooner was she fairly installed in her new home than she announced that she would give a ball, and the wives of all the other men who were working on the railroad were invited, and so were every other man's wife.

The first society of Atlanta was there, and it was a swell affair, or we thought it was. Mrs. Mulligan was mistress of ceremonies, and she said that I would have to dance the first set with her. I had on a pair of rough hightopped boots, but that gave Mrs. Mulligan no concern. She said that it did not matter at all, at all. We circled around a few times, and the heel of one of my boots got cought in the floor, and the heel came off. I finished the dance in a hippity-hop sort of fashion, but, as they say now-a-days, everything went then. It was a creme de la creme affair, and the function established Mrs. Mulligan as the leader of the four hundred. She was quite a fine looking woman of strong physique, and if anybody had questioned her leadership she could have established her claim to the championship as well as to the leadership.

But you know how women are about things. If one has something her neighbor wants it too. Well, sir, the day after the ball a delegation of the men came to me, and announced that their wives wanted plank floors in their shacks, and they declared that if I didn't put them in the houses every blessed man of them would quit work.

I had to send out to Collier's Mill and get a good many loads of puncheons to floor the other shacks. That is the history of the first social function that ever occurred in Atlanta (then Terminus) after the Indians left this county....

RAILROADS COME TO ATLANTA - 1845

Despite Mrs. Mulligan's "ball," Terminus was a pioneer town. Its permanent settlers needed more than the rough and tumble justice of a railroad camp, and on December 23, 1843, a town charter was granted. The new entity was called Marthasville, after the daughter of Georgia's governor, but it remained backward and isolated until the tracks of the Georgia Railroad entered the community.

Source: The Atlanta Journal, December 15, 1883.

In 1845 Marthasville was too small to be called a village. The four, now principal, streets of the city were then straggling country roads, and the only clearing of any importance was right at their junction. Only about twelve or fourteen families resided here, and the entire population was estimated to be about one hundred souls. The dwellings were mostly log cabins, such as to-day may be seen on the frontier in the West. On the south-west corner of Marietta and Peachtree streets stood a small grocery store, owned by Jonathan Norcross; fronting this stood Kile's grocery store, and down near where the Markham House now stands was a grocery store kept by Collins & Loyd. In the rear of the Republic block, on Pryor street, stood a two-story frame building which was used by the officers of the Western and Atlantic railroad. On Peachtree street, near the site of the First Methodist Church, stood a small, wooden building, used as a school-house, church and public hall. These were the most notable features of that time. On the 15th of September, 1845, the Georgia Railroad was completed to Augusta, and the first through train came to Marthasville, bearing Judge John P. King, the president of the road, and several other railway magnates and distinguished persons. The scene in the neighborhood of the depot can better be imagined than described. Almost the whole population were present, and the wildest excitement prevailed. Farmers in the country, for forty miles around, had heard of the advent of the iron horse, for days, and when the time arrived they were on hand in force. Some came in one-ox carts, with their families, and from the supply of provisions which they brought it was evident that they intended to have a jubilee. Atlanta has had bigger crowds, but never one so wild and delirious with excitement. The locomotive was eagerly inspected, the cars were examined inside and out, the engineer and fireman were interviewed, the conductor was looked upon as a hero, the president of the road and the other distinguished gentlemen were heartily welcomed. The enthusiasm of the people knew no bounds, and in accordance with the times a mass meeting was held. The place chosen was about a half a mile northwest of the depot, Walton Spring. The names of the speakers have not been handed down to this generation, but among them was Colonel John M. Clark, the father of our will-known fellow citizen, Colonel E. Y. Clark. An old gentleman who was present at this meeting informed the writer that the address was a masterpiece of eloquence and created tremendous enthusiasm. The speaker pictured, in a prophetic way, the future of Atlanta, dwelt upon the importance of commercial facilities, and speaking of the Georgia road, said, that its completion had 'tied the ocean to the hills....'

ATLANTA BEGINS TO GROW - 1847

The railroads guaranteed the success of Atlanta. Once track was laid into town, the community began to attract settlers like Dr. William White, who sought to "establish myself here while the place is new." In his Diary, White described the rough and bustling town of 1847.

Source: Atlanta Centennial Year Book, 1837-1937. (Atlanta, 1937), 45-48.

October 21, 1847. In the center of the northern part of the State of Georgia lies the county of DeKalb, of which the county seat is Decatur. Six miles west of it in the midst of oak and chestnut forests, is the city of Atlanta. I suppose it can hardly be found on the map, for nineteen months ago the first dwelling was commenced. It lies at the junction of three great railroads: The State, leading off to the Tennessee river and thence connected by steam-boat with the Mississippi, -- the Central leading down to Macon and Savannah; and the Georgia to Augusta and Charlotte; -- the connecting at Augusta with Savannah by steamboats. The city contains 2,500 inhabitants, thirty large stores; two hotels, that would accommodate 150 each; three newspapers; and two schools, one of them taught by a gentleman, and the other by a lady, who teaches A.B.Cs.; 187 buildings have been put up this summer within eight months, and more are in progress. The woods all around are full of shanties, and the merchants live in them until they can find time to build. The streets are still full of stumps and roots; large chestnut and oak logs are acattered about, -- but the streets are alive with people and the stores full of trade, and bustle. Not a church has yet been built, though the Baptists, Methodists and Episcopalians have each one ready to raise in a short time. Preaching is held in the railroad depot, and in the school houses, or "academies" -- as they are called.

I have thought then that I could not do better than establish myself here while the place is new and so grow up with the people. It is close to the Allegheney Mountains and consequently cool and healthy. All northern fruits are raised in the county adjacent and so are all northern crops. Nearly half of the population are northern men. Board is cheap, only $8 a month, and three scholars in the higher branches would board me for a year. There are lots of children who I am assured would go to school worth patronizing, and from what I can see I am sure with a good building in a very short time I could make a thousand dollars a year. But there is the difficulty, the only building I can get is a miserable shell of a thing without ceiling and it can not be finished this winter. I have been to all prominent men of the place, who promise their influence, and those who have children, their patronage. For two years there will be great difficulties on account of the unfixed character of the inhabitants; the poverty of most of the present settlers, and this year the discomforts of the old building.

The cotton picking season has just commenced and it comes in at the rate of 50 or 60 wagon loads a day. This is nothing to what it will be in December, and it will continue until Spring; like the butter up north it is brought here to market from places 100 miles distant. Grain and all such supplies come down from the entire Cherokee country, the most populous section of Georgia. I believe the place will be about the size of Utica, N.Y., eventually, and hence I think I shall stay here....

There are several beautiful springs in the village and the water is good; -- the land is rolling. There are not 100 negroes in the place, and white men black their own shoes, and dust their own clothes, as independently as in the north. All through the upper part of Georgia the labor is done almost entirely by white hands. Carpenters get but ten shillings a day here, and labor commands about the same price as at the north. Tuition is $12, $16, $24, and $32 a year, according to what they study.

I have only been here two days and am becoming quite an old settler. The people here bow and shake hands with everybody they meet, as there are so many coming in all the time that they cannot remember with whom they are acquainted.

It is cool enough for a fire today; two very slight frosts have occurred this month: leaves are turning a very little; -- walnuts and chestnuts are ripe. I have given up eating Irish potatoes since I left New York, as I like the sweet ones so much better. They cook them in a dozen ways, in puddings, in pies, custards, as well as baked. They make capital corn bread, but they always set wheat bread on the table, too -- biscuits, batter cakes, etc. -- beef and chicken are the meats. I like the fare very much.

The health of the place is excellent; they have coughs, colds and consumption occasionally, and especially up in the mountains. Below us the diseases are mostly bilious....

Saturday, October 23. Went about today and and obtained in all twenty-nine scholars, -- shall have thirty at least to commence with, and as the people are all favorably disposed to me, all I have to do is to sustain myself, which with God's blessing I trust I shall be able to do. Saw Frost of Decatur and he thinks there will be little difficulty in establishing myself, though at first the profits will be small. As the other fellow is a lawyer he will not have the same inducements to incite him as will actuate me -- whose all is staked upon the venture.

Frost thinks that I have a much better prospect than he had, and last year he cleared $800. As scholars advance in Algebra and Latin, $32 a year counts up, and I am sure in a year or two to have just as much business as I want.

Sunday, October 24th. We have as yet in Atlanta no city law or charter. The nights are full of noise and commotion which a city government would easily repress. Last night I was very much disturbed by these noises. No preaching here today. It does not seem like the Sabbath, except that the stores are closed.

Monday, October 25th. I have found the proprietor of the bookstore a very pleasant companion. He has welcomed me very kindly to his store, and I spend my leisure time reading there. His name is McPherson from Franklin College, Tennessee. He proposed for me to room with him in the counting room, and I think I will enjoy the arrangement very much. I have been reading "Holmes' Southern Gardener, " various works on Southern husbandry and horticulture generally. There is a great lack of a Southern original work on botany. Nothing but Eaton's large work will supply the defiency. If I had means and money I should go into it extensively and shall yet, if some one does not anticipate me there.

Saturday, October 30th. Was present this evening at the meeting of the citizens of Atlabta to petition for a City Government. Captain Loyd was in the chair. Mr. Bartlett, the printer, was the secretary. A committee of Colonel Collier, Dr. Bomar, Dr. Smith, Jonathan Norcross, and Thurmond were appointed to draft a bill of incorporation for the city. Atlanta now contains 2,000 inhabitants, yet every one does what is right in his own eyes. There is no government and it is wonderful that they are as steady as they are at present; no minister, no church and little preaching; a Sabbath school is in successful operation and that is almost the only religious privilage that is enjoyed.

I may consider myself one of the fathers of the City; -- being present at its birth. A meeting could not be conducted with a more complete disregard to order than the one last night. Half a dozen motions were at once before the house....

November 2. The cotton crop this year is unusually large. It is thought there will be at least half a million bales or two million pounds more than ever before. But it is of no avail, the greater the crop always the less the price and the failures in Europe are enough of themselves to bring the price down. Cotton has declined since I have been here, from nine and one-half to six cents, and will hardly bring that. When cotton goes down negroes, food, plantation, city property, everything in the whole south goes with it, -- to rise again as soon as the great staple increases in value.

Business here is daily increasing. Several thou sand dollars worth per diem are purchased of cotton, corn, wheat, etc., and the whole business of the place so far is cash, so that the growth is healthy. New stores are continually being opened. I am satisfied, however, that only on the outskirts will Atlanta ever be beautiful: five railroads are enough to spoil the ground plan and regularity of any place whatsoever. The greater part of the development lie on either side of the Augusta railroad.

We have a pretty name for our place. We are indebted for it to John C. Calhoun, who contemplates if the "Union is dissolved" making it the seat of government. It is the central point of the south, and when the railroads to Nashville and Montgomery are completed it will be the most accessible both from the east and west of the whole southern part of the Union. A great railroad meeting is to be held with delegates from eight states on the 23rd of this month. Many of the most distinguished men of the south will be present....

MORALITY TRIUMPHANT - 1851

In December, 1847, the Georgia Legislature approved a charter for the City of Atlanta. The town boundaries were enlarged, and a Mayor/Council form of Government was established. The new city still retained its pioneer qualities, and railroad men were a constant threat to law and order. They tended to congregate in "Snaketown" and "Murrel's Row," where whiskey and women were available. Yet growing numbers of "respectable" citizens intended to build a community where they could happily raise their children. The election campaign of 1850-51 was a battle between the "rowdy" "moral" factions. The aftermath of "moral" victory was described by Thomas H. Martin, Builders of Atlanta :

Source: Thomas H. Martin, Builders of Atlanta (Atlanta: Century Publishing Co., 1902), I, 90-93.

There were over forty drinking saloons in the place, to say nothing of the groceries that dealt in ardent refreshments, and it goes without saying that they all did a landoffice business while the great political war raged. While Simpson and his backers were turning their money loose in the barrooms, Jonathan Norcross and his friends, to emphasize the moral plane on which they were fighting, treated liberally to apples and confectionery. The Moral Party held several big rallies at which the leaders denounced the corruption and disorder existing in Atlanta, and called upon the better element to rescue the city from rowdyism and vice. The Rowdy Party held no mass meeting, but an outlet was not wanting for their enthusiasm. Happily the election passed off without any fatalities, resulting in the election of Jonathan Norcross as mayor of Atlanta.

It had been the boast of the most turbulent spirits in the Rowdy Party that "uncle Jonathan" would find the town too hot to hold him, if he tried to execute his proposed reforms, and in more than one instance he had been threatened with personal violence. It was part of the mayor's duties to hold police court, there being no municipal recorder at that time. Mayor Norcross had been in office but a day or two when he was called upon to try a burly ruffian who had been arrested for an affray on the street. Trouble was expected at the hearing as some of the most dangerous Murrellites were suspected of plotting to do the new mayor harm by getting themselves arrested and attacking him in open court. The city government then had its headquarters in a second story room of the building afterward occupied by the dry goods establishment of John Keely. A large crowd was present to witness the mayor's first case, and a large part of the spectators were by no means sympathetic. The case proceeded with due formality, and as the evidence was conclusive, Mayor Norcross fined the bully and was about to proceed with the next case when the fellow suddenly rose from his chair, as the officers were advancing to his side to take him to the calaboose, and drew a wicked-looking bowie knife with a blade at least a foot long. Flourishing the weapon over his head, the prisoner loudly defied any man in the court room to take him and declared that he proposed to start a slaughter pen right there. At that he started to cut and slash right and left with his big knife, the crowd falling over each other in their frightened efforts to get down the stairway. Allen E. Johnson, the sheriff of DeKalb county, was present in the room, as were City Marshal William McConnell, and Deputy Marshal Benjamin N. Williford. C.H. Strong joined these officers in their effort to cope with the desperate man. As for Mayor Norcross, he quickly sprang from his old splint-bottom chair, and raising it high above his head in in a defensive attitude awaited the attack of the desperado, having no better weapon. It was evident that the man was intent at getting at the mayor. Sheriff Johnson always carried a stout hickory cane, and in this emergency it stood him in good stead. He aimed a blow with his cane at the hand held knife, and a second later the knife was ringing on the floor and the hand in a fit condition for a poultice. Sheriff Johnson and Mr. Strong then seized the prisoner and disregarding the scowling faces of his friends, who had not the nerve to carry out their conspiracy, hustled him down stairs into the street. By this time it was dark, court having been called late in the afternoon, and the prisoner managed to escape amid the jostling crowd in the darkness. He was never seen again in Atlanta.

The next day the town was at fever pitch of excitement, and everybody felt that serious trouble was imminent. Business was practically suspended, and the men of both factions gathered in groups and talked threateningly. There were several hundred unsavory characters in the Rowdy Party who, it was feared, would not scruple to raise a bloody riot, and the more timid of the respectable element were talking seriously of leaving town. Among the majority of the latter, however, the sentiment was strong for organizing a vigilance committee if the machinery of municipal government was inadaquate to cope with the grave situation. The next night the Rowdy Party took the belicose initiative. In the village of Decatur was a small, ancient cannon, a relic of the War of 1812, which the townsfolk were wont to fire on Fourth of July and other occasions of public jubilation. This the "rowdies" obtained by some means, the next night, and planted in front of Jonathan Norcross's store, with the muzzle trained upon the building. They fired it off two or three times, but it was only loaded with sand and gravel, and no damage was done, save dirtying Norcross's porch. The outlaws left a written notice, however, to the effect that Mayor Norcross must either resign or leave town, or they would return and blow up his store. This lawless act was not interfered with by the city authorities, the marshal and his assistants keeping at a discreet distance, and none of the Moral Party showing themselves. But the next day there was no shrinking on the part of the good citizens. The mayor called a secret meeting of the council, which resulted in his issuing a proclamation calling upon all law-abiding citizens to form themselves at once into a volunteer police force to aid in securing the enforcement of the local laws. The response of the Moral Party was immediate and determined. Citizens assembled in front of the Norcross store with their guns and pistols, and all day the work of organizing them into a volunteer police force proceeded quietly. Trouble was espected after nightfall. The Rowdy Party also perfected a warlike organization during the day, meeting in force in a house on Decatur street, near where the Willingham building now stands.

The old cannon had been left in the middle of the street at the four corners, as a menace to Norcross's store, but the desperate "sporting fraternity" did not muster courage to return and put their threat into execution. Had they done so, a hand-to-hand battle would have been fought right there, for the Moral Party was guarding the vicinity, at least a hundred strong, and its guard and patrols were scattered all over the town. At midnight, there being evidently no danger of an attack by the Rowdy Party, a large squad of the volunteer police, under the leadership of A. W. Mitchell, was detailed to move upon headquarters of the enemy in the building spoken of on Decatur street. There were several squads, commanded by the leaders of well-known courage appointed by the mayor and council, and these moved upon other low quarters of the town where the rowdies rendezvoused. Before this show of courageous force the Rowdy Party dissolved like frost in the warm breath of the sun. Not a man, for all their former bluster, stood his ground, but the whole unsavory lot slunk like coyotes to their holes, except such as fell into the hands of the volunteer police as they were attempting to escape. Some fifteen or twenty rowdy ringleaders, however, remained in the Decatur street house too long, and when they attempted to flee, found the houses surrounded. They were arrested, without offering any resistance and conducted by a large armed force to the little calaboose, where they were locked up. As the place would not hold all the prisoners, only the worst ones were thrust inside and the rest strongly guarded in a private building.

The cases against the captured rowdies were set for the next day, and the whole town turned out at the trial, the street in front of the city hall being choked with people. One after another the offenders were convicted and fined to the limit allowed by the charter, and in default of the fine, most of them were remanded to jail. This broke the backbone of the "rebellion," though for several weeks unusual vigilance and energy was required on the part of the municipal authorities to preserve order, and the whole volunteer police force was not disbanded for some time. During the rest of his administration Mayor Norcross was not molested, but he received several anonymous threats through the mail and the feeling against him in Murrell's Row was dangerously vindictive.

THE MINUTE MAN ASSOCIATION - 1860

The newly christened "Gate City" continued to grow as the shadow of Civil War fell across the nation. Almost ten thousand citizens lived in Atlanta by 1860, and almost all were offended when Stephen A. Douglas visited their city in October and exhorted them to support the Union. Atlanta's "true Southern men" responded by organizing the pro-South Minute Man Association.

Source: Wallace P. Reed, History of Atlanta (Syracuse, 1889), 96-97.

WHEREAS, It is now probable and almost certain that an Abolition candidate will be elected to the chief magistracy of the Union upon the avowed and undisguised declaration on his part and on the part of his supporters, that this common government shall be administered for the destruction of the rights and of the Southern States in the Union, and

WHEREAS, We recognize the right of any sovereign State to withdraw from the partnership of States whenever in her sovereign capacity she may determine that the objects of the Confederacy have been perverted, or not carried out in good faith, therefore,

Resolved, That we as citizens of Georgia acknowledge our allegiance to our State as paramount to our allegiance to the Federal government, and that in the event of the election of Abraham Lincoln, we pledge ourselves to maintain at all hazards, and to the last extremity any course that may be adopted for self-defense against the Federal power.

Resolved, That if any Southern State may determine to secede from the Union we will by all means in our power assist her in resistance against any effort on the part of a black Republican administration to coerce her back into the Confederacy.

Resolved, That it is the sacred duty of Southern men in the present alarming crisis to forget past political differences and to unite together, as brethren of one household, in determined opposition to the policy of a black Republican party.

The above resolutions were seconded by Colonel T. C. Howard. Thomas L. Cooper eloquently supported the resolutions, and in the course of his speech said that in case of Lincoln's election he would do all in his power to induce Georgia to secede from the Union. At the close of his remarks he offered the following as supplementary to the above resolutions:

We, the undersigned, hereby agree to unite ourselves into an association to be called the Minute Men Association of Fulton County. This object we propose to accomplish.

First. By using all lawful and honorable means to bring about the peaceable secession of the State of Georgia from the Union, in the contingency above named.

Second. By giving moral and national aid to the citizens of any other Southern State which may secede in the contingency above named, and which the Federal government may attempt to coerce back into the Union.

Third. By using all lawful and honorable means under the sanction of our State, to unite our people as a band of brothers in resistance to Northern aggression, and in defense of ourselves, our property and our firesides against Federal power wielded by a black Republican administration.

For the accomplishment of the purposes above named we hereby pledge ourselves, and cordially invite men of all parties to join us, much preferring independence out of the Union to dishonor, degradation and oppression within it.

SHERMAN TAKES ATLANTA - 1864

As the Civil War began, Atlanta was already the hub of the South. The city's strategic importance was recognized by both sections and after the abortive "Andrews Raid" of 1862, the Confederacy placed it under martial law. For the rest of the War, Atlanta was the South's major distribution point as well as a hospital center. Its rear-echelon status ended when General William Tecumseh Sherman moved his armies toward Atlanta in May, 1864. His brilliant campaign would ultimately devastate the Gate City.

Source: Memoirs of General W.T. Sherman, an autobiographical account (New York: Charles L. Webster and Co., 1890), 108-109, 166-179.

.... General Slocum had reached his corps (the Twentieth), stationed at the Chattahoochee bridge, had relieved General A.S. Williams in command, and orders had been sent back to him to feel forward occasionally toward Atlanta, to observe the effect when we had reached the railroad. That night I was so restless and impatient that I could not sleep, and about midnight there arose toward Atlanta sounds of shells exploding, and other sound like that of musketry. I walked to the house of a farmer close by my bivouac, called him out to listen to the reverberations which came from the direction of Atlanta (twenty miles to the north of us), and inquired of him if he had resided there long. He said he had, and that these sounds were just like those of a battle. An interval of quiet then ensued, when again, about 4 A.M., arose other similar explosions, but I still remained in doubt whether the enemy was engaged in blowing up his own magazines, or whether General Slocum had not felt forward, and become engaged in a real battle.

The next morning General Hardee was gone, and we all pushed forward along the railroad south, in close pursuit, till we ran up against his lines at a point just above Lovejoy's Station. While bringing forward troops and feeling the new position of our adversary, rumors came from the rear that the enemy had evacuated Atlanta, and that General Slocum was in the city. Later in the day I received a note in Slocum's own handwriting, stating that he had heard during the night the very sounds that I have referred to; that he had moved rapidly up from the bridge about daylight, and had entered Atlanta unopposed. His letter was dated inside the city, so there was no doubt of the fact. General Thomas's bivouac was but a short distance from mine, and, before giving notice to the army in general orders, I sent one of my staff-officers to show him the note. In a few minutes the officer returned, soon followed by Thomas himself, who again examined the note, so as to be perfectly certain that it was genuine. The news seemed to him too good to be true. He snapped his fingers, whistled, and almost danced, and, as the news spread to the army, the shouts that arose from our men, the wild hallooing and glorious laughter, were to us a full recompense for the labor and toils and hardships through which we had passed in the previous three months.

A courier-line was at once organized, messages were sent back and forth from our camp at Lovejoy's to Atlanta, and to our telegraph-station at the Chattahoochee bridge. Of Course, the glad tidings flew on the wings of electricity to all parts of the north, where the people had patiently awaited news of their husbands, sons, and brothers, away down in "Dixie Land;" and congratulations came pouring back full of good-will and patriotism. This victory was most opportune; Mr. Lincoln himself told me afterward that even he had previously felt in doubt, for the summer was fast passing away; that General Grant seemed to be checkmated about Richmond and Petersburg, and my army seemed to have run up against an impassable barrier, when, suddenly and unexpectedly came the news that "Atlanta was ours, and fairly won." On this text many a fine speech was made, but none more eloquent than that by Edward Everett, in Boston. A presidential election then agitated the North. Mr. Lincoln represented the national cause and General McClellan had accepted the nomination of the Democratic party, whose platform was that the war was a failure, and that it was better to allow the South to go free to establish a separate government, whose corner-stone should be slavery. Success to our arms at that instant was therefore a political necessity; and it was all-important that something startling in our interest should occur before the election in November.... I knew that an army which had penetrated Georgia as far as Atlanta could not turn back. It must go ahead, but when, how, and where, depended on many considerations. As soon as Hood had shifted across from Lovejoy's to Palmetto, I saw the move in my "mind's eye;" and, after Jeff. Davis's speech at Palmetto, of September 26th, I was more positive in my conviction, but was in doubt as to the time and manner. When General Hood first struck our railroad above Marietta, we were not ready, and I was forced to watch his movements further, till he had "carromed" off to the west of Decatur. Then I was perfectly convinced, and had no longer a shadow of doubt. The only possible question was as to Thomas's strength and ability to meet Hood in the open field. I did not suppose that General Hood, though rash, would venture to attack fortified places like Allatoona, Resaca, Decatur, and Nashville; but he did so, and in doing so he played into our hands perfectly.

On the 2d of November I was at Kingston, Georgia, and my four corps -- the Fifteenth, Seventeenth, Fourteenth, and Twentieth -- with one division of cavalry, were strung from Rome to Atlanta. Our railroads and telegraph had been repaired, and I deliberately prepared for the march to Savannah, distant three hundred miles from Atlanta. All the sick and wounded men had been sent back by rail to Chattanooga; all our wagon-trains had been carefully overhauled and loaded, so as to be ready to start on an hour's notice, and there was no serious enemy in our front....

The greatest possible attention had been given to the artillery and wagon trains. The number of guns had been reduced to sixty-five, or about one gun to each thousand men, and these were generally in batteries of four guns each.

Each gun, caisson, and forge, was drawn by four teams of horses. We had in all about twenty-five hundred ambulances, with two horses to each. The loads were made comparatively light, about twenty-five hundred pounds net; each wagon carrying in addition the forage needed by its own team. Each soldier carried on his person forty rounds of ammunition, and in the wagons were enough cartridges to make up about two hundred rounds per man, and in like manner two hundred rounds of assorted ammunition were carried for each gun....

I reached Atlanta during the afternoon of the 14th, and found that all preparations had been made -- Colonel Beckwith, chief commissary, reporting one million two hundred thousand rations in possession of the troops, which was about twenty days' supply, and he had on hand a good supply of beef-cattle to be driven along on the hoof. Of forage, the supply was limited, being of oats and corn enough for five days, but I knew that within that time we would reach a country well stocked with corn, which had been gathered and stored in cribs, seemingly for our use, by Governor Brown's militia.

Colonel Poe, United States Engineers, of my staff, had been busy in his special task of destruction. He had a large force at work, had leveled the great depot, round-house, and the machine-shops of the Georgia Railroad, and had applied fire to the wreck. One of these machine-shops had been used by the rebels as an arsenal, and in it were stored piles of shot and shell, some of which proved to be loaded, and that night was made hideous by the bursting of shells, whose fragments came uncomfortably near Judge Lyon's house, in which I was quartered. The fire also reached the block of stored near the depot, and the heart of the city was in flames all night, but the fire did not reach the parts of Atlanta where the court-house was, or the great mass of dwelling-houses.

The march from Atlanta began on the morning of November 15th, the right wing and cavalry following the railroad southeast toward Jonesboro', and General Slocum with the Twentieth Corps leading off to the east by Decatur and Stone Mountain,... I remained in Atlanta during the 15th with the Fourteenth Corps, and the rear guard of the right wing, to complete the leading of the trains, and the destruction of the buildings of Atlanta which could be converted to hostile uses, and on the morning of the 16th started with my personal staff,...

About 7 A.M. of November 16th, we rode out of Atlanta by the Decatur road, filled by the marching troops and wagons of the Fourteenth Corps; and reaching the hill, just outside of the old rebel works, we naturally paused to look back upon the very ground whereon was fought the bloody the bloody battle of July 22nd, and could see the copse of wood where McPherson fell. Behind us lay Atlanta, smouldering and in ruins, the black smoke rising high in the air, and hanging like a pall over the ruined city. Away off in the distance, on the McDonough road, was the rear of Howard's column, the gun-barrels glistening in the sun, the white-topped wagons stretching away to the south; and right before us the Fourteenth Corps, marching steadily and rapidly, with a cheery look and swinging pace, that made light of the thousand miles that lay between us and Richmond. Some band. by accident, struck up the anthem of "John Brown's soul goes marching on;" the men caught up the strain, and never before or since have I heard the chorus of "Glory, glory, hallelujah!" done with more spirit, or in better harmony of time and place.

Then we turned our horses' heads to the east; Atlanta was soon lost behind the screen of trees, and became a thing of the past. Around it clings many a thought of desperate battle, of hope and fear, that now seem like the memory of a dream; and I have never seen the place since.

ATLANTA BEGINS TO REBUILD - 1865

The Union armies left Atlanta a ruined city, two-thirds burned, its rail lines destroyed, its population decimated. In time its devastation was to become a mirror of the defeated South. After Appomattox, reporters traveled across the Confederacy and in November, 1865 one of the most perceptive northern visitors described Atlanta.

Source: Sidney Andrews, <u>The South Since the War</u> (Boston: Ticknor and Fields, 1866), 338-343.

Atlanta is built on something less than a hundred hills; and, excepting Boston, is the most irregularly laid out city I ever saw. In fact, the greater portion of it seems never to have been laid out at all till Sherman's army came in here. That did the work pretty thoroughly, -- so thoroughly, indeed, as to prove remarkable destructive ability in his men.

Coming here has dispelled two illusions under which I rested: first, that Atlanta was a small place; and second, that it was wholly destroyed. It was a city of about fourteen thousand inhabitants two years ago, and it was not more than half burned last fall. The entire business portion, excepting the Masonic Hall building and one block of larger residences in all parts of the city were also burned. But the City Hall and the Medical College, and all the churches, and many of the handsomer and more stylish private dwellings, and nearly all the houses of the middling and poorer classes, were spared; and on the first of last June there was ample shelter here for at least six or eight thousand persons. Of course, however, when the entire business portion of the place had disappeared, the city had been practically put out of the way for the time being, even if nothing be said of the fact that it was depopulated by military orders.

The marks of the conflict are everywhere strikingly apparent. The ruin is not so massive and impressive as that of Columbia and Charleston; but as far as it extends it is more complete and of less value. The city always had a mushroom character, and the fire-king must have laughed in glee when it was given over into his keeping. There is yet abundant evidence of his energy, -- not so much in crumbling walls and solitary chimneys, as in thousands of masses of brick and mortar, thousands of pieces of charred timber, thousands of half-burned boards, thousands of scraps of tin roofing, thousands of pieces of charred timber, thousands of car and engine bolts and bars, thousands of ruined articles of hardware, thousands upon thousands of tons of <u>debris</u> of all sorts and shapes. Moreover, there are plenty of cannon-balls and long shot lying about the streets, with not a few shell-struck houses in some sections; and from the court-house square can be seen a dozen or more forts, and many a hillside from which the timber was cut so that the enemy might not come upon the city unawares.

From all this ruin and devastation a new city is springing up with marvellous rapidity. The narrow and irregular and numerous streets are alive from morning till night with drays and carts and handbarrows and wagons, -- with hauling teams and shouting men, -- with loads of lumber and loads of brick and loads of sand, -- with piles of furniture and hundreds of packed boxes, -- with mortar-makers and hod-carriers, -- with carpenters and masons, -- with rubbish removers and house-builders, -- with a never-ending throng of pushing and crowding and scrambling and eager and excited and enterprising men, all bent on building and trading and swift fortune-making.

Chicago in her busiest days could scarcely show such a sight as clamors for observation here. Every horse and mule and wagon is in active use. The four railroads centring here groan with the freight and passenger traffic, and yet are unable to meet the demand of the nervous and palpitation city. Men rush about the streets with little regard for comfort or pleasure, and yet find the days all too short and too few for the work in hand. The sound of the saw and plane and hammer rings out from daylight till dark, and yet master-builders are worried with offered contracts which they cannot take. Rents are so high that they would seem fabulous on Lake Street, and yet there is the most urgent cry for store-room and office-room. Four thousand mechanics are at work, and yet five thousand more could get immediate employment if brick and lumber were to be had at any price. There are already over two hundred stores, so called, and yet every day brings some trader who is restless and fretful till he secures a place in which to display another stock of goods.

Where all this eagerness and excitement will end no one seems to care to inquire. The one sole idea first in every man's mind is to make money. That this apparent prosperity is real no outsider can believe. That business is planted on sure foundations no merchant pretends. That there will come a pause and then a crash, a few prudent men prophesy.

Meantime Atlanta is doing more than Macon and Augusta combined. The railroad from here to Chattanooga clears over one hundred thousand dollars per month, and could add fifty thousand more to that enormous sum if it had plenty of engines and rolling stock. The trade of the city is already thirty per cent greater than it was before the war, and it is limited only by the accommodations afforded, and has even now spread its wings far out on streets heretofore sacred to the privacy of home....

ATLANTA: THE PHOENIX - 1871

Like the mythical Phoenix, Atlanta rose from its ashes stronger and more powerful than before. Although many were wedded to the myths of the "Lost Cause," the rebirth of the city and the renewal of its spirit were evident by 1871.

Source: John Stainback Wilson, Atlanta As It Is (New York: Little, Rennie and Co., 1871), 18-81.

The general plan of Atlanta is beautiful, being a perfect circle, with the centre near the Passenger Depot. But the plan of the streets is not so good. Indeed, the streets do not appear to be laid off with any regard to system or order. They turn about in various ways, and cross each other at every kind of angle. The location and direction of old roads seem to have had more to do with the course of the streets than anything else; and it might be said that the plan of the streets is about this: -- Where you find a road, take it. The streets are also rather narrow, but not enough so to have any injurious effect on health, with the advantages of thorough drainage, pure air, good water, and proper attention to sanitary measures.

But, on account of the growing population and business of the city, it is greatly to be regretted that other streets were not widened, after the war, as was that beautiful thoroughfare appropriately called Broad Street. Marietta is also a wide and beautiful street; but Peachtree and Whitehall are too narrow for the demands made on them. When the street railroads, which will soon doubtless be built, are laid down, the want of sufficient width in our principal streets will be considerable inconvenience. But let us have the railroads at all hazards. And in this connection it affords me great pleasure to add, that present indications are favorable for the early completion of one or two important and much needed lines of street railroads. Atlanta should certainly have street railroads, when cities of less trade and enterprise have these conveniences.... Does Atlanta offer any inducements as a health resort? Yes, many. Some of these may be mentioned: -- Her accessibility is unexcelled; the climate is mild; the water pure; the air invigorating; all the necessaries and luxuries of life are reasonable in price; the private boarding and hotel accomodations are excellent; and the social, religious, and educational advantages are all that could be desired. With such inducements as these, is it too much to say that the day is not far distant when this highly favored city will become the very Mecca of invalids -- a place of resort for thousands from the East and the West, from the North and the South, who will make their offerings to the beauteous Goddess of Health here enshrined? Here, where it is too high up for malarious deseases, such as fevers of various kinds, and too low down for mountainous diseases, such as consumptions, rheumatisms, etc. --

here, on these health-crowned hills, this lovely Goddess delights to dwell....

Allusion having just been made to the social, religious and educational advantages of Atlanta, this is a very proper place to speak more fully on the society, etc. In a new place like this, to which people from all quarters have been attracted soon after a great revolution which well-nigh over-turned the social, moral, and political institutions of the whole country, the society is, of course composed of heterogeneous elements. But, notwithstanding the denunciation that has been heaped on Atlanta, as a sink of moral pollution and a seething hot-bed of political corruption, it may be safely stated that the moral and social condition of this city will compare favorably with most other cities, old or new, North or South....

On Whitehall Street are some fine blocks. The most prominent building on this street is James's six-story store -- the tallest, and among the finest in the city. We are also indebted to the owner, Mr. John H. James, for the finest private residence in Georgia. This house has been recently sold to the State, as a residence for the Governor, and is well worthy of a description, did space permit. Mr. James, with his characteristic enterprise, is making arrangements to build another fine private residence, which will be an ornament to the city, and a monument of his liberality and good taste....

De Give's has already been mentioned as the principal place of amusement in Atlanta. With twenty-eight churches, and only one or two places of public amusement, it would seem that our citizens are more of a church-going than a theatre-going people. Some idea of the moral condition of the city may be formed from this state of things....

ATLANTA'S BLACK POPULATION - 1881

Community life was not pleasant for Atlanta's black population. A reporter from the Constitution dutifully described the misery in one of those areas during 1881. Most Atlantans, however, ignored black poverty and emphasized Atlanta's growth.

Source: The Atlanta Constitution, July 19, 1881.

Few people in Atlanta ever stop to consider how the colored people of the city live. We see them every day; they are about us and work for us, and at night go to their homes; but what these homes are and where they are, and the little picture that each hearthstone presents, we never think of. There is, however, an attachment between many employers and the negroes whom they employ, which springs naturally, and in many instances leads to numerous little acts on the part of the employer which help to smooth the path for the dependent colored brother to pass over. But by far the largest proportion of negroes are never really known to us. They are not employed in private homes, nor in the business houses, but drift off to themselves, and are almost as far from the white people, so far as all practical benefits of association are concerned, as if the two races never met.

A study of this class of our population is most interesting. Yesterday, a Constitution reporter, while sitting in the arcade of the Kimball, conceived the idea of writing up briefly some of the most prominent haunts and homes of these people. Sallying forth, he drifted down the shady side of Decatur Street to the rear of the handsome block of buildings which front the Kimball, where he found the first negro establishment which was to come under his observation. It was a negro barber shop, and inside some eight or ten men, who, a few years ago, were slaves, were submitting their beards to the tonsorial artists with all the free and easy style of professional bloods.

But the reporter grew tired and turned away from the barber pole establishment and drifted on down to the corner of Ivy. It was nearly sundown and the street was packed with colored people of every size and class -- big, little, old, young, black, yellow, mad, happy, sad, men, boys, women, girls, all together in such a squirm of confusion as to require an expert to make his way along the sidewalk in anything like a satisfactory manner. As usual an ice cream vendor had gone into camp at the corner, and at regular intervals of thirty seconds his lusty voice could announce that he was disposing of ice cream of an unsurpassed quality, 'cold and hard.'

A little way down Ivy Street the reporter encountered the odor of frying fish -- an almost sure sign of a negro lunch house. There are hundreds of these little six by nine establishments over the city, where the whole stock in trade amounts to a boiled ham, the ever-present fired fish and bread to go along. These lunch houses are generally the essence of filth, but there are some that are quite decent. One in particular furnishes many white families with bread.

But the reporter pushed his way further still until he peeped into the rear room of the Willingham building, and stood face to face with a colored undertaker's establishment. Here the pauper coffins are made -- plain pine boxes in which are borne to the potter's field the unfortunates who die in poverty.... How different are the funerals this old man attends from those where wealth and position provide long lines of carriages. No monuments are reared over over the graves he makes, yet the pauper in his plain pine box, may find in an unmarked grave a rest as sweet as falls to him who sleeps beneath a marble shaft.

But the reporter recovered his mental equilibrium and moved on to the unpoetic Beaver Slide, a delectable locality at the rear of the Wilmingham Building. The Beaver Slide is a succession of small houses, one-story in height, all touching and covering a lot probably 150 feet fronting on Ivy street. The rooms are the smallest imaginable, and, with the numerous inhabitants, filth and general repulsiveness, present a picture that beggars description. Aside from the sleeping rooms there are several front rooms devoted to business. The restaurant is there, together with a shoe shop, and further on down is a negro billiard room and a beer saloon. Here by the light of a few smoky oil lamps, and to the soul-harrowing music of a string band, the colored beaux and dusky damsels, who rarely speak to a white person, trip the light fantastic toe, not forgetting to refresh themselves at the saloon counter when each dance is ended. The manner in which this place received its name is not known and can only be a matter of surmise. Judge Richard H. Clark, who reaches conclusions by a reasoning route, says that the name was given because of the great amount of passing in and out there like at the beaver slides on the banks of a creek.

The Ant Hole was once a negro den in that locality, which gave the police no small amount of trouble. It was the room under the building at the northeast corner of Ivy and Decatur, and was certainly one of the worst places in the city. Negroes of the very worst type would congregate there and play cards, smoke and drink. It was a fit place to bear a harvest of criminals and doubtless many daring crimes had their conception there. It is now, however, in the hands of good men and is in every way a satisfactory place.

Another place that does no credit to the locality is at the corner of Decatur and Collins streets. Here worthless negroes congregate, and a little further up Collins, at the Karwisch barracks the negroes live under a very bad state of affairs.

Over in the rear of the fourth ward is Shermantown and Ellis Row, where worthless negroes and still more worthless whites live in the same neighborhood and sometimes in the same houses. Mechanicsville and Hell's Half Acre, out to the left of Whitehall Street, were once very bad localities, but have improved their morals.

Fuller's Row and Campbell's Block, on the Central Railroad are two big negro neighborhoods, and from there one drops softly into Happy Hollow, a famous locality on Peters Street between Castleberry's hill and the barracks. Bone Alley and Pigtail Alley also contribute a share of colored citizens when there is any fun up. Happy Hollow, is the home of George McKinney, a noted colored politician.

Near the Central railroad crossing is another Campbell block. This is a lot about 150 feet square, twelve feet below the street and supplied with a semi-circle of negro cabins, in the center of which is a shed, under which, in true Lycurgus style, are the common implements of the laundry where all wash clothes harmoniously together until some sister gets in a bad humor....

There can be no doubt that some of these dens, some of poverty, and some of vice, are the nests where the worst forms of crime are born and bred, and every true Atlantan must long for the good time coming when they will be choked out of existence by the demand for Atlanta space....

THE NEW SOUTH - 1886

Without doubt, Atlanta represented the type of Southern mentality most acceptable to north-business leaders. One spokesman for sectional rapproachment was Henry Grady, editor of the <u>Constitution.</u> On December 21, 1886 he was invited to be the first southerner to address the New England Society. Inspired by the presence of General Sherman, he gave voice to the aspirations of the "New South."

Source: Edward DuBois Shurter (ed.), <u>The Complete Orations and Speeches of Henry Grady</u> (Norwood, Massachusetts: South-west Publishing Co., 1910) 14-19.

I want to say to General Sherman, who is considered an able man in our parts, though some people think he is a kind of careless about fire, that from the ashes he left us in 1864 we have raised a brave and beautiful city; that somehow or other we have caught the sunshine in the bricks and mortar of our homes, and have builded therein not one ignoble prejudice or memory.

But what is the sum of our work? We have found out that in the summing up the free negro counts more than he did as a slave. We have planted the schoolhouse on the hilltop and made it free to white and black. We have challenged your spinners in Massachusetts and your ironmakers in Pennsylvania. We have learned that the $400,000,000 annually received from our cotton crop will make us rich when the supplies that make it are home-raised. We have reduced the commercial rate of interest from 24 to 6 per cent, and are floating 4 per cent bonds. We have learned that one Northern immigrant is worth fifty foreigners, and have smoothed the path to Southward, wiped out the place where Mason and Dixon's line used to be, and hung out the latchstring to you and yours.

We have reached the point that marks perfect harmony in every household, when the husband confesses that the pies which his wife cooks are as good as those his mother used to bake; and we admit that the sun shines as brightly and the moon as softly as it did before the war. We have established thrift in city and country. We have fallen in love with work. We have restored comfort to homes from which culture and elegance never departed.... Above all, we know that we have achieved in these "piping times of peace" a fuller independence for the South than that which our fathers sought to win in the forum by their eloquence or compel in the field by their swords.

It is a rare privilege, sir, to have had part, however humble, in this work. Never was nobler duty confided to human hands than the uplifting and upbuilding of the prostrate and bleeding South -- misguided, perhaps, but beautiful in her suffering, and honest, brave, and generous always. In the record of her social, industrial, and political illustration we await with confidence the verdict of the world.

But what of the negro? Have we solved the problem he presents or progressed in honor and equity toward solution? Let the record speak to the point. No section shows a more prosperous laboring population than the negroes of the South, none in fuller sympathy with the employing and land-owning class. He shares our school fund, has the fullest protection of our laws, and the friendship of our people. Self-interest, as well as honor, demand that he should have this. Our future, our very existence, depend upon our working out this problem in full and exact justice. We understand that when Lincoln signed the Emancipation Proclamation, your victory was assured, for he then committed you to the cause of human liberty, against which the arms of man cannot prevail -- while those of our statesmen who trusted to make slavery the corner stone of the Confederacy doomed us to defeat as far as they could, committing us to a cause that reason could not defend or the sword maintain in sight of advancing civilization.

Had Mr. Toombs said, which he did not say, "that he would call the roll of his slaves at the foot of Bunker Hill," he would have been foolish, for he might have known that whenever slavery became entangled in war it must perish, and that the chattel in human flesh ended forever in New England when your fathers -- not to be blamed for parting with what didn't pay -- sold their slaves to our fathers -- not to be praised for knowing a paying thing when they saw it. The relations of the Southern people with the negro are close and cordial. We remember with what fidelity for four years he guarded our defenseless women and children, whose husbands and fathers were fighting against his freedom. To his eternal credit be it said that whenever he struck a blow for his own liberty, he fought in open battle, and when at last he raised his black and humble hands that the shackles might be struck off, those hands were innocent of wrong against his helpless charges, and worthy to be taken in loving grasp by every man who honors loyalty and devotion. Ruffians have maltreated him, rascals have misled him, philanthropists established a bank for him, but the South, with the North, protests against injustice to this simple and sincere people.

To liberty and enfranchisement is as far as law can carry the negro. The rest must be left to conscience and common sense. It must be left to those among whom his lot is cast, with whom he is indissolubly connected, and whose prosperity depends upon their possessing his intelligent sympathy and confidence. Faith has been kept with him, in spite of calumnious assertions to the contrary by those who assume to speak for us or by frank opponents. Faith will be kept with him in the future, if the South holds her reason and integrity.... The South found her jewel in the toad's head of defeat. The shackles that had her in narrow limitations fell forever when the shackles of the negro slave were broken. Under the old regime the negroes were slaves to the South; the South was a slave to the system. The old plantation, with its simple police regulations and feudal habit, was the only type possible under slavery. Thus was gathered in the hands of a splendid and chivalric oligarchy the substance that should have been diffused among the people, as the rich blood, under certain artificial conditions, is gathered at heart, filling that with affluent rapture, but leaving the body chill and colorless.

The old South rested everything on slavery and agriculture, unconscious that these could neither give nor maintain healthy growth. The new South presents a perfect democracy, the oligarchs leading in the popular movement; a social system compact and closely knitted, less splendid on the surface, but stronger at the core; a hundred farms for every plantation, fifty homes for every palace; and a diversified industry that meets the complex needs of this complex age.

THE "ATLANTA COMPROMISE" - 1895

Henry Grady hoped for a racially harmonious South whose business interests could integrate her into the national economy. No one individual's endorsement was more influential in achieving that ideal than that of Booker T. Washington. When the International Cotton Exposition opened, Washington delivered his "Atlanta Compromise" oration. No less a commentator than President Cleveland decided the "Exposition would be fully justified if it did no more than furnish the opportunity" for Washington's speech.

Source: <u>Address of Booker T. Washington ... delivered at the opening of the Cotton States and International Exposition at Atlanta, Georgia, September 18, 1895</u> (Atlanta, 1895).

MR. PRESIDENT AND GENTLEMEN OF THE BOARD OF DIRECTORS AND CITIZENS:

One third of the population of the South is of the Negro race. No enterprise seeking the material, civil, or moral welfare of this section can disregard this element of our population and reach the highest success. I but convey to you, Mr. President and Directors, the sentiment of the masses of my race when I say that in no way have the value and manhood of the American Negro been more fittingly and generously recognized than by the managers of this magnificent Exposition at every stage of its progress. It is a recognition that will do more to cement the friendship of the two races than any occurence since the dawn of our freedom.

Not only this, but the opportunity here afforded will awaken among us a new era of industrial progress. Ignorant and inexperienced, it is not strange that in the first years of our new life we began at the top instead of at the bottom; that a seat in Congress or the State Legislature was more sought than real estate or industrial skill; that the political convention or stump speaking had more attractions than starting a dairy farm or truck garden.

A ship lost at sea for many days suddenly sighted a friendly vessel. From the mast of the unfortunate vessel was seen a signal: "Water, water; we die of thirst!" The answer from the friendly vessel at once came back: "Cast down your bucket where you are." A second time the signal, "Water, water; send us water!" ran up from the distressed vessel, and was answered: "Cast down your bucket where you are." And a third and fourth signal for water was answered: "Cast down your bucket where you are." The captain of the distressed vessel, at last heeding the injunction, cast down his bucket, and it came up full of fresh, sparkling water from the mouth of the Amazon River. To those of my race who depend on bettering their condition in a foreign land, or who underestimate the importance of cultivating friendly relations with the Southern white man, who is their nest door neighbor, I would say: "Cast down your bucket where you are" -- cast it down in making friends in every manly way of the people of all races by whom we are surrounded.

Cast it down in agriculture, mechanics, in commerce, in domestic service, and in the professions. And in this connection it is well to bear in mind that whatever other sins the South may be called to bear, when it comes to business, pure and simple, it is in the South that that the Negro is given a man's chance in the commercial world, and in nothing is this Exposition more eloquent than in emphasizing this chance. Our greatest danger is, that in the great leap from slavery to freedom we may overlook the fact that the masses of us are to live by the productions of our hands, and fail to keep in mind that we shall prosper in proportion as we learn to dignify and glorify common labor and put brains and skill into the common occupations of life; shall prosper in proportion as we learn to draw the line between the superficial and the substantial, the ornamental gewgaws of life and the useful. No race can prosper till it learns that there is as much dignity in tilling a field as in writing a poem. It is at the bottom of life we must begin, and not at the top. Nor should we permit our grievances to overshadow our opportunities.

To those of the white race who look to the incoming of those of foreign birth and strange tongue and habits for the prosperity of the South, were I permitted I would repeat what I say to my own race, "Cast down your bucket bucket where you are." Cast it down among the 8,000,000 Negroes whose habits you know, whose fidelity and love you have tested in days when to have proved treacherous meant the ruin of your firesides. Cast down your bucket among these people who have without strikes and labor wars, tilled your fields, cleared your forests, built your railroads and cities, and brought forth treasures from the bowels of the earth, and helped make possible this magnificent representation of the progress of the South. Casting down your bucket among my people, helping and encouraging them as you are doing on these grounds, and to education of head, hand, and heart, you will find that they will buy your fields, and run your factories. While doing this, you can be sure in the future, as in the past, that you and your families will be surrounded by the most patient, faithful, law-abiding, and unresentful people that the world has seen. As we have proved our loyalty to you in the past, in nursing your children, watching by the sick bed of your mothers and fathers, and often following them with tear-dimmed eyes to their graves, so in the future, in our humble way, we shall stand by you with a devotion that no foreigner can approach, ready to lay down our lives, if need be, in defense of yours, interlacing our industrial, commercial, civil, and religious life with yours in a way that shall make the interests of both races one. In all things that are purely social we can be as separate as the fingers, yet one as the hand in all things essential to mutual progress.

There is no defense or security for any of us except in the highest intelligence and development of all. If anywhere there are efforts tending to curtail the fullest growth of the Negro, let these efforts be turned into stimulating, encouraging, and making him the most useful and intelligent citizen. Effort or means so invested will pay a thousand per cent interest. These efforts will be twice blessed -- "blessing him that gives and him that takes."

There is no escape through law of man or God from the inevitable:

> The laws of changeless justice bind
> Oppressor with the oppressed;
> And close as sin and suffering joined
> We march to fate abreast.

Nearly sixteen millions of hands will aid you in pulling the load upwards, or they will pull against you the load downwards. We shall constitute one third and more of the ignorance and crime of the South, or one third its intelligence and progress; we shall contribute one third to the business and industrial prosperity of the South, or we shall prove a veritable body of death, stagnating, depressing, retarding every effort to advance the body politic.

Gentleman of the Exposition, as we present to you our humble effort at an exhibition of our progress, you must not expect overmuch. Starting thirty years ago with ownership here and there in a few quilts and pumpkins and chickens (gathered from miscellaneous sources), remember the path that has led from these to the inventions and production of agricultural implements, buggies, steam engines, newspapers, books, statuary, carving, paintings, the management of drug stores and banks has not been trodden without contact with thorns and thistles. While we take pride in what we exhibit as a result of our independent efforts, we do not for a moment forget that our part in this exhibition would fall far short of your expectations but for the constant help that has come to our educational life, not only from the Southern States, but especially from Northern philanthropists, who have made their gifts a constant stream of blessing and encouragement.

The wisest among my race understand that the agitation of questions of social equality is the extremest folly, and that progress in the enjoyment of all the privileges that will come to us must be the result of severe and constant struggle rather than of artificial forcing. No race that has anything to contribute to the markets of the world is long in any degree ostracized. It is important and right that all privileges of the law be ours, but it is vastly more important that we be prepared for the exercises of these privileges. The opportunity to earn a dollar in a factory just now is worth infinitely more than the opportunity to spend a dollar in an opera house.

In conclusion, may I repeat that nothing in thirty years has given us more hope and encouragement, and drawn us so near to you of the white race, as this opportunity offered by the Exposition; and here bending, as it were, over the altar that represents the results of the struggles of your race and mine, both starting practically empty-handed three decades ago, I pledge that in your effort to work out the great and intricate problem which God has laid at the doors of the South you shall have at all times the patient, sympathetic help of my race; only let this be constantly in mind that, while from representations in these buildings of the product of field, of forest, of mine, of factory, letters, and art, much good will come, yet far above and beyond material benefits will be that higher good, that let us pray God will come, in a blotting out of sectional differences and racial animosities and suspicions, in a determination to administer absolute justice, in a willing obedience among all classes to the mandates of law. This, coupled with our material prosperity, will bring into our beloved South a new heaven and a new earth.

W.E.B. DUBOIS ON BLACK EDUCATION IN ATLANTA - 1905

Ten years after the "Atlanta Compromise" of Booker T. Washington, a new militancy was apparent among black educators. At Atlanta University, the restricted vocational role defined by Washington was rejected and a new educational philosophy was presented.

Source: William Edward Burghardt DuBois, From Servitude to Service (Atlanta, 1906).

.... There are very few institutions in the United States really doing college work for Negroes. Many institutions called colleges represent an ambition or an ideal, while as a matter of present fact such schools are higher institutions simply in name; in reality they are great primary and grammar schools with a score of high school students and a few or none of college grade. They represent, in many cases, high hopes and laudable ambition, but in some cases they have no present prospect or design of developing into real colleges, and in some other cases they have been tempted to be content with calling a high school a college, possibly after the venerable example of Harvard in its early days. This practice, however, has led to the suspicion that all Negro colleges are of low rank and parading more or less under false pretenses.

There are in the United States to-day about five institutions which, by reason of the number of students and grade of work done, deserve to rank as Negro colleges. How far, now, is the work done at an institution like Atlanta University deserving of the respect due to liberal training?

If there is one thing at Atlanta University upon which we pride ourselves it is that we have never succumbed to the temptation of mere numbers. We have to-day seventy-five students of a rank above the high school -- fifty in the regular college course, and twenty-five in the teacher's college. It is fair to say that we might, by a general lowering of standard, easily have a college of one hundred to one hundred and fifty. This we have steadily refused to do. On the contrary, we have sought unceasingly, year by year, to raise and fix a fair standard, and I think it is perfectly just to say that so far as our work goes in Atlanta University, the standard equals that of any New England school. We have a high school of two hundred and twenty-five pupils, divided into two parallel courses of three years, an English and classical. This gives one year less than the New England high schools with their four-year courses.... certainly the influence of Atlanta University has been a most potent factor. In the work of Negro uplift throughout the land our graduates are not alone nor altogether singular -- graduates of a score of of other worthy institutions are working with them, but the long, thorough courses of study in our work, the unbending mental discipline as a foundation for all work, whether manual or intellectual, has left its enduring mark on the Atlanta University man. The work of these college trained men from this and other institutions is not to be judged simply by what they have done, but still more from what they have prevented. I am persuaded that Americans do not dwell enough on this side of the case. You complain of crime and vagrancy among Negroes, and both are large and threatening, as it is perfectly natural they should be, but consider what they might have been if this race had been left without leaders--not leaders who could simply read and write and hoe, but real thinkers, men of vision, men who realized the tremendous import of this vast social movement and could stand ever ready within the veil to calm passion and direct energy and say to the turbulent waters, "Peace be still."

The peculiar character of work, however, makes Atlanta University more than a simple college -- it is a social settlement where, for six or seven years, the best we can find of the growing generation of Negroes is brought into contact with the standards of modern culture in school and home and campus. Nor do we wish to stop here -- the Social Settlement aims to do more than teach the slums; it seeks also by studying slums to teach the world what slums mean. And Atlanta University seeks to become a centre for the careful, earnest and minute study of the Negro problems, through the experience and active cooperation of other graduates scattered all over the south. For this purpose we have established a department of social inquiry and an Annual Conference to study the Negro problem.... Being by birth and education a southern man, I could but look with critical eye, and really with some distrust, upon this attempt to confer the higher education upon the Negro, but the years have left me with no doubt as to the wisdom of all that has been done. It has been a noble and a successful work. With scant means and under great difficulties, the consecrated men in control have accomplished much direct good for the Negro, with a valuable reflex influence upon the white people.

The active open opposition to our work has long since disappeared and here and there men who accidentally or through their daily work have been brought into contact with us have not hesitated to testify to its value. After all, the opposition to higher training for Negroes is not usually based on actual knowledge of its results, but rather upon its supposed inherent and theoretical absurdity when viewed as a policy; and back of such view, hidden or clouded, forgotten or artfully concealed, sits the real unspoken thing that prompts the oposition (sic) -- namely, the feeling that black men are not men. There is no doubt of the unfortunate spread of anti-Negro prejudice in the North in recent years. There is no doubt of the spread of the caste spirit, even beyond the color line. This is a national calamity and calls for something more than exclamations and sighs on your part. It is not surely too much to ask that parents and teachers of the future citizens of the nation should see to it that they themselves are broad enough and honest enough and brave enough and brave enough to recognize human desert and accomplishment under any human guise and to teach their pupils and children to do likewise; for this is no passing difficulty; no merely local problems; nothing of even simply national concern. We have a way in America of wanting to be rid of problems. It is not so much a desire to reach the best and largest solution as it is to clear the board and start a new game. Of this, our most sinister social problem, the future status and development of 9,000,000 Negroes, most Americans are simply tired and impatient. They do not wnat to solve it; they do not want to understand it; they want simply to be done with it and hear the last of it. Of all possible attitudes this is the most significant fact of the opening century, namely, that the Negro problem in America is but a local phase of a world problem, "The problem of the Twentieth Century is the problem of the color line."

THE RIOT OF 1906 - 1906

The problems of the "color line" became intolerable in time, and in September 1906, the rage of repressed blacks eruped in violence. Neither speeches nor fire hoses could halt the rampage, and almost 100 casualties resulted. A Citizens Report on the riot was published in the Constitution and is reprinted in Walter G. Cooper, History of Fulton County.

Source: Walter G. Cooper, History of Fulton County (Atlanta, 1934), 827-829.

"1. Among the victims of the mob there was not a single vagrant.
"2. They were earning wages in useful work up to the time of the riot.
"3. They were supporting themselves and their families or dependent relatives.
"4. Most of the dead left small children and widows, mothers or sisters, with practically no means, and very small earning capacity.
"5. The wounded lost from one to eight weeks' time, at fifty cents to four dollars a day each.
"6. About seventy persons were wounded, and among those there was an immense amount of suffering. In some cases, it was prolonged and excruciating pain.
"7. Many of the wounded are disfigured, and several are permanently disabled.
"8. Most of them were in humble circumstances, but they were honest, industrious and law-abiding citizens and useful members of society.
"9. These statements are true of both white and colored.
"10. Of the wounded ten are white and sixty are colored. Of the dead two are white and ten are colored, two female and ten male. This includes three killed at Brownsville.
"11. Wild rumors of a large number killed have no foundation that we can discover. As the city was paying for funeral expenses of victims, and relief was given their families, they had every motive to make known their loss. In one case relatives of a man killed in a broil made fruitless efforts to secure relief.
"12. Two persons reported as victims of the riot had no connection with it. One, a negro man, was killed in a broil over a crap game, and another, a negro woman, was killed by her paramour. Both homicides ocurred at some distance from the scene of the riot.
"13. As twelve persons were killed and seventy were murderously assaulted, and as by all accounts, a number took part in each assault, it is clear that several hundred murderers or would-be murderers are at large in this community.

"14. Although less than three months have passed since the riot, events have already demonstrated that the slaughter of the innocent does not deter the criminal class from committing more crime. Rape and robbery have been committed in the city and suburbs during that time.

"15. The slaughter of the innocent does drive away good citizens. From one small neighborhood twenty-five families have gone. A great many of them were buying homes on the installment plan.

"16. The crimes of the mob include robbery as well as murder. In a number of cases the property of innocent and unoffending people was taken. Furniture was destroyed, small shops were looted, windows were smashed, trunks were burst open, money was taken from the small hoard, and articles of value were appropriated. In the commission of these crimes the victims, both men and women, were treated with unspeakable brutality.

"17. As the result of four days of lawlessness there are in this glad Christmas time widows of both races mourning for their husbands, and husbands of both races mourning for their wives; there are orphan children of both races who cry out in vain for faces they will see no more; there are grown men of both races disabled for life, and all this sorrow has come to people who are absolutely innocent of any wrong-doing.

"In conclusion, we call attention to the fact that up to this time Atlanta has been a law-abiding city, and criminals of all kinds, with a single exception, had been punished by legal methods. Repeatedly, in view of hundreds of men, the sheriff has conducted along the public highways, prisoners charged with the most odious crimes, and these prisoners have had legal trials, which resulted in the punishment of the guilty and the aquittal of the innocent.

"Considering this record of a law-abiding community, it is amazing that the things we have recited could have happened in Atlanta, and that the small minority which constitutes the tough element was allowed to crucify this community in the eyes of the world, and shock the moral sense of our own people.

SEGREGATION IN ATLANTA - 1908

The riot indicated that Atlanta, despite its "New South" rhetoric, remained preeminently a southern city. Its white citizens' attitudes and opinions had been forged by a lifetime of unquestioning discrimination. The reality of life in Atlanta is apparent in this selection.

Source: Ray Stannard Baker, Following the Color Line (New York: Doubleday, Page & Co., 1908), 26-311, 34-38, 49, 65.

...I set out from the hotel on the morning of my arrival to trace the colour line as it appears, outwardly, in the life of such a town.

Atlanta is a singularly attractive place, as bright and new as any Western city. Sherman left it in ashes at the close of the war; the old buildings and narrow streets were swept away and a new city was built, which is now growing in a manner not short of astonishing. It has 115,000 to 125,000 inhabitants, about a third of whom are Negroes, living in more or less detached quarters in various parts of the city, and giving an individuality to the life interesting enough to the unfamiliar Northerner. A great many of them are always on the streets far better dressed and better-appearing than I had expected to see -- having in mind, perhaps, the tattered country specimens of the penny postal cards. Crowds of Negroes were at work mending the pavement, for the Italian and Slav have not yet appeared in Atlanta, nor indeed to any extent anywhere in the South. I stopped to watch a group of them. A good deal of conversation was going on, here and there a Negro would laugh with great good humour, and several times I heard a snatch of a song; much jollier workers than our grim foreigners, but evidently not working so hard. A fire had been built to heat some of the tools, and a black circle of Negroes were gathered around a drop of molasses and they were all talking while they warmed their shins -- evidently having plenty of leisure.

As I continued down the street, I found that all the drivers of waggons and cabs were Negroes; I saw Negro newsboys, Negro porters, Negro barbers, and it being a bright day, many of them were in the street -- on the sunny side.

I commented that evening to some Southern people I met, on the impression, almost of jollity, given by the Negro workers I had seen. One of the older ladies made what seemed to me a very significant remark.

"They don't sing as they used to," she said. "You should have known the old darkeys of the plantation. Every year, it seems to me, they have been losing more and more of their care-free good humour. I sometimes feel that I don't know them any more. Since the riot they have grown so glum and serious that I'm free to say I'm scared of them!"

One of my early errands that morning led me into several of the great new office buildings, which bear testimony to the extraordinary progress of the city, And here I found one of the first evidences of the colour line for which I was looking. In both buildings, I found a separate elevator for colored people....

I found that no Negro ever went into an elevator devoted to white people, but that white people often rode in cars set apart for coloured people. In some cases, all the elevators in a building are operated by coloured men. This is one of the curious points of industrial contact in the South which somewhat surprise the Northern visitor. In the North a white workman will often refuse to work with a Negro; in the South, while the social prejudice is strong, Negroes and whites work together side by side in many kinds of employment....

One of the points in which I was especially interested was the "Jim Crow" regulations, that is, the system of separation of the races in street cars and railroad trains. Next to the question of Negro suffrage, I think the people of the North have heard more of the Jim Crow legislation than of anything else connected with the Negro problem. The street car is an excellent place for observing the points of human contact between the races, betraying as it does every shade of feeling upon the part of both. In almost no other relationship do the races come together, physically, on anything like a common footing....

I was curious to see how the system worked out in Atlanta. Over the door of each car, I found this sign:

> WHITE PEOPLE WILL SEAT FROM FRONT OF CAR TOWARD THE BACK AND COLORED PEO- PLE FROM REAR TOWARD FRONT

Sure enough, I found the white people in front and the Negroes behind. As the sign indicates, there is no definite line of division between the white seats and the black seats, as in many other Southern cities. This very absence of a clear demarcation is significant of many relationships in the South. The colour line is drawn, but neither race knows just where it is. Indeed, it can hardly be definitely drawn in many relationships, because it is constantly changing. This uncertainty is a fertile source of friction and bitterness. The very first time I was on a car in Atlanta, I saw the conductor -- all conductors are white -- ask a Negro woman to get up and take a seat farther back in order to make a place for a white man. I have also seen white men requested to leave the Negro section of the car....

After I had begun to trace the colour line I found evidences of it everywhere -- literally in every department of life. In the theatres, Negroes, with the result that coloured people have their own eating and sleeping places, many of them inexpressibly dilapidated and unclean. "Sleepers wanted" is a familiar sign in Atlanta, giving notice of places where for a few cents a Negro can find a bed or a mattress on the floor, often in a room where there are many other sleepers, sometimes both men and women in the same room crowded together in a manner both unsanitary and immoral. No good public accommodations exist for the educated or well-to-do Negro in Atlanta, although other cities are developing good Negro hotels. Indeed one cannot long remain in the South without being impressed with extreme difficulties which beset the exceptional coloured man.

In slavery time many Negroes attended white churches and Negro children were often taught by white women. Now, a Negro is never (or rarely) seen in a white man's church. Once since I have been in the South, I saw a very old Negro woman, some much-loved mammy, perhaps -- sitting down in front near the pulpit, but that is the only exception to the rule that has come to my attention. Negroes are not wanted in white churches. Consequently the coloured people have some sixty churches of their own in Atlanta. Of course, the schools are separate, and have been ever since the Civil War....

Right in this connection: while I was in Atlanta, the Art School, which in the past has often used Negro models, decided to draw the colour line there, too, and no longer employ them.

Formerly Negroes and white men went to the same saloons, and drank at the same bars, as they do now, I am told, in some parts of the South. In a few instances, in Atlanta, there were Negro saloon-keepers, and many Negro bartenders. The first step toward separation was to divide the bar, the upper end for white men, the lower for Negroes. After the riot, by a new ordinance no saloon was permitted to serve both white and coloured men.

Consequently, going along Decatur Street, one sees the saloons designated by conspicuous signs:*

"WHITES ONLY"   "COLOURED ONLY"

And when the Negro suffers the ordinary consequences of a prolonged visit to Decatur Street, and finds himself in the city prison, he is separated there, too, from the whites. And afterward in court, if he comes to trial, two Bibles are provided; he may take his oath on one; the other is for the white man. When he dies he is buried in a separate cemetery....

THE LORDS OF COCA-COLA - 1910

While ignorance and hardship might well be the lot of the average Atlanta worker, regardless of color, the leadership of the city was firmly held by a business elite that fostered prosperity and growth. In this stratum of society, no family was more important than the Candlers, and no company more influential than Coca-Cola. A reporter recalled the almost royal privileges accorded both these Atlanta institutions.

Source: Thomas Stokes, <u>Chips Off My Shoulder</u> (Princeton, 1940), 28-31.

There was one professor in high school who was so bold as to poke around in the social stream of Atlanta. His daily stint was ancient and medieval history which seemed to bore him as it did us. His heart was not much in it. But he had an outside hobby -- and his heart was in that. This was the inequitable tax system of the city, inequitable as the politicians administered it. His chief complaint was the favortism shown our Coca-Cola millionaire, Asa G. Candler, who, he said, paid taxes on a very negligible valuation on the pride and joy of our growing city, the twenty-one-story Candler Building on Peachtree Street, while the average man was taxed closely to the value of his property. Looking back, I don't know how he was permitted such heresy. His study had been thorough and exhaustive. I guess his enthusiasm had to spill over in revelation. I suppose he did not fear that second-grade high school students would be much concerned. He just had to talk to someone. It left an impression on one youthful mind which could have been impressed by more facts about the world in which we live -- had someone taken the trouble to explore and tell.

The Candlers, being then our outstanding wealthy family, were treated reverentially by press and pulpit -- and by the city government. They had achieved, because the palate of America had taken to a five-cent drink that was stimulating. Asa Candler had risen in the good old American way -- as did Henry Ford later -- by devising a cheap product for the masses. Until fairly well along in life he had been a small-time druggist, as Henry Ford had been a small-time mechanic with an idea. There was luck in it, of course. We often forget that, as we bow down to the "enterprise and initiative" of our capitalists.

Atlanta was the Candlers and Coca-Cola, and the Candlers and Coca-Cola were Atlanta. So the city was known afar. It is of course, toying with the truth to say Atlanta was a city built by a soft drink, but the soft drink contributed much to its fame and fortune, and the Candlers were our royal family and a dominent influence in our city life of that day. Asa Candler was interviewed about civic affairs and business conditions. We elected him mayor once on a "reform" wave, one of those occasions when the populace is convinced that what the city needed was to take it away from the "politicians" and have a "business administration by a businessman." Subsequently, of course, we handed it back to the politicians. The Candlers developed their eccentricities, some of them, and some of them were involved in the usual troubles that come to plague the rich. Even Asa, himself, became involved in a breach-of-promise suit by a New Orleans beauty who supplied his ardent love letters -- he was well along in years then -- to the court and the public. Vicariously we enjoyed these troubles that only the rich can afford. After all, it was our royal family, and it was nice to have them human and amusing.

The family's prestige was elevated -- and somewhat protected -- by the presence of a bishop, Bishop Warren A. Candler, a brother of Asa, a powerful man of the cloth in one of the most powerful Protestant flocks of Georgia and the South, the Methodists. His dictum was law ecclesiastically -- and in other ways. The bishop pointed the way for the donation of his brother's soft-drink millions to church and education and great was the name of Candler in my time.

It was a potent combination of wealth and religion. Deep into Georgia's economy and politics did its influence spread. As the business grew, as the fountain of never-ceasing nickels leaped higher and higher, it showered riches upon other men and, in time, really big capital bought it out and raised up still other millionaires. (In every family was the knowing one who claimed that he knew he should have bought Coca-Cola stock way back -- and look where the family would be now, on Easy Street. He would shake his head sadly. For some had gambled on it, and he could point out their ornate residences and sweeping lawns.) It was only natural that Coca-Cola should enter politics to keep its taxes down and protect its various interests, and this it did.

Cola-Cola (sic) speaks effectively in Georgia politics today. It is one of the sacred business institutions, along with the Georgia Power Company, and the textile mills which are sprinkled about the state.

I was something of this which my high school teacher was hinting to us. I have learned all about it since....

ZONING IN ATLANTA - 1922

On May 21, 1917, a devasting fire swept Atlanta. It laid waste to 300 acres, destroyed $5,000,000 in property and made refugees of 10,000 citizens. Faced once again with the prospect of rebuilding from the ashes, Atlanta created a city planning commission. In 1922 a zoning plan was proposed and quickly adopted. The very idea of was new to the South, so the document had educational as well as professional ramifications. Social realism was evidenced by its explicit racial segregation.

Source: Robert Whitten, The <u>Atlanta Zone Plan</u> (Atlanta City Planning Commission, 1922), 8-10.

Zoning will conserve property values. Haphazard development is bound to be costly and uneconomic development. Zoning will save enormous waste in building construction. With uncontrolled building development the construction of a new building in a neighborhood often means a net loss in the aggregate value of the building of that neighborhood. With zoning, each new building increases the aggregate value in an amount equal to and usually in excess of its own cost.

Zoning will attract money to a city for investment in real estate. Large lending institutions will be inclined to favor those cities in which their investments will be afforded the safeguard of a comprehensive zoning plan. Failure to provide the zoning safeguard is as inexcusable as failure to protect property against destruction by fire.

Zoning protects the home. Quiet and freedom from the distraction incident to trade, industry and attendant street traffic are essential to a wholesome home environment.

Zoning will establish uniform building lines in the residence sections, thus giving opportunities for a front lawn with a lawn and trees and preventing one building from pushing out in front of its neighbors.

Zoning will promote industrial development. It will set aside adequate areas for industries within which the new plant may locate without incurring the criticism and continual complaints of neighboring residents and owners. It will atrract to the city and to the home areas near the industrial areas a good and abundant labor supply. The segregation of industries wil make it possible to serve the industrial areas more effectively and more econonomically with sewers, trucking routes and freight facilities.

Zoning promotes the health and comfort of the people. Orderly city growth cannot fail to have a marked effect on the physical fitness and vitality of the city's inhabitants. . . .

The two classes of residence districts are:
  Class U1 or dwelling house district.
  Class U2 or apartment house district.

A building arranged for more than two families may not be constructed in a dwelling house district. One of the chief purposes of the zone plan is to preserve Atlanta as a city of homes. While a certain number of apartment houses are beneficial, they should not be allowed to drive out the private homes in all sections of the city. Carefully limited but adequate areas are allowed for apartment house development. The dwelling house districts, from which apartment houses are excluded, will include the larger portion of the entire area of Atlanta.

Trade and industry are excluded from the residence districts. Churches, schools, libraries, etc., are permitted in the residence districts. Hospitals, sanitariums and institutional buildings are permitted in those blocks of the residence districts already occupied by similar buildings.

The residence districts are further subdivided into three race districts:
  R1 or white residence district.
  R2 or colored residence district.
  R3 or undetermined race district.

In the white residence districts no house not occupied by a colored family at the time of the passage of the zoning ordinance can be thereafter occupied by a colored family. In the colored residence districts no house not occupied by a white family at the time of the passage of the zoning ordinance can be thereafter occupied by a white family. Servants quarters located on the same lot as the residence they serve will nevertheless be allowed in either district without distinction as to race. Certain limited residence areas are placed in neither the white district nor the colored district but are left undetermined as to the race zoning.

The above race zoning is essential in the interest of the public peace, order and security and will promote the welfare and prosperity of both the white and colored race. Care has been taken to prevent discrimination and to provide adequate space for the expansion of the housing areas of each race without encroaching on the areas now occupied by the other. . . .

THE VIADUCT SYSTEM - 1929

Atlanta also quickly adjusted to the motor car. By March 1929, a system of bridges and viaducts had been constructed to expedite both automobile traffic and railroad commerce. Forty years later the boutiques and restaurants of "Underground Atlanta" opened under part of the viaduct system.

Source: J. Henson Tatum, "Atlanta Builds Its Viaducts," The City Builder,(April, 1929), 1 1, 47.)

    Atlanta's greatest viaduct job is finished. The new Pryor Street and Central Avenue bridges, with their laterals, are open to traffic. Pent-up flow of vehicles in Peachtree, Whitehall and other principal downtown streets is greatly relieved. Like water released through a spillway, traffic has sought the viaducts. They are channels of uninterrupted flow, efficient outlets for streams of traffic that have heretofore coursed at stagnant pace through the central district.

    The two viaducts and their laterals, if placed end to end, would form a bridge one mile long, lacking only 122 feet. . . .

    Total cost of the project, including preliminary work (the railroad tracks from east of Piedmont Avenue to west of Forsyth Street had to be lowered from 5 to 6 feet) and property adjustments, is approximately $ 2,225,000. The bridges were financed by proceeds from sale of bonds (issue of 1926), and contributions by Fulton County. The steam railroads and electric railway directly benefited by their erection.

    Atlanta citizens voted a bond issue of $ 1,000,000 for the bridges. The Georgia Power Company contributed $ 400,000; county of Fulton, $386,068; Georgia Railroad, $230,600; and N.C. & St. L. Railway, $167,075. Bonds of the million-dollar issue netted a premium of $41,624, which sum was also appropriated to the enterprise. . . .

    Briefly stated, the viaduct project accomplishes the following benefits, among others:

1. Relieves downtown traffic congestion.
2. Abolishes two railroad grade crossings (for many years the busiest in the city).
3. Permits trains to proceed into and out of Union Station without halting and without uncoupling.
4. Banishes hazard to motorists and pedestrians which was formerly present at the grade crossings.
5. Does away with railroad and public delay.
6. Remakes large area into more attractive district.
7. Enhances property usefulness and property values.

8. Completes the linking of north and south sides
9. Provides improved approach to Fulton County court house and new city hall.
10. Opens new street car routes through city. . . .

THE ATLANTA HOUSING AUTHORITY-1938

Like all great American cities, Atlanta suffered greatly during the depression years 1929-1939. Hard times changed areas of the proud "City of Homes" into festering ghettoes. New Deal programs took up the task of renewal, and Atlanta's Techwood Homes became the model for urban housing projects. Atlanta's own Housing Authority was created to deal with the problem of rebuilding Atlanta.

Source: Housing Authority of the City of Atlanta, Georgia. Second Annual Report, June 30, 1940, (Atlanta, 1940), 4-5, 11.

Atlanta, justly proud of her many fine and beautiful homes and her neat, well-kept cottages, has other houses within her borders which are far different from those for which she is famed.

These other houses--shacks without sanitary facilities, old barn-like buildings without safe or adequate heating and lighting equipment, or badly overcrowded dwellings below the standard of safety, decency or health--house more than one-third of the city's population. According to the government Social and Economic Survey, at least 39% of the people in Atlanta live in substandard houses.

To get a true picture of the conditions under which these people were living, it was necessary to go into the substandard houses of the city. It was necessary to see the sagging doors, the dark holes where plaster had fallen from the walls, to watch the rats, to see how families were living doubled-up with half enough beds, to observe that several families used a common cold water faucet and shared an outdoor privy, to smell the musty odors which are ever present in houses where there are no facilities and little incentive for cleanliness.

Only recently has Atlanta become conscious of the extent to which housing evils exist. And only recently has the public realized tha danger of allowing the slums to spread unheeded and unchecked.

Recent surveys made by the Federal Government have conclusively proved what was only suspected before--that slums constitute a real menace to the entire population of a city. As each item was checked, it was found that the same areas in the city produced the highest death rate, the greatest amount of disease, the largest number of crimes, arrests and juvenile delinquency cases, the most fires. These areas invariably coincided with those most thickly covered with substandard houses.

The fact that 37% of the fires in the city were occurring in the 20% of the city where substandard houses greatly predominated was significant. The fact that 56% of all deaths in the city occurred in the 39% of the population which lived in slum areas was startling. As the evidence piled up, the seriousness of the situation became apparent. It was found that 57% of infant deaths, 69% of deaths from tuberculosis, occurred in the slums. Sixty-one per cent of the bed patients treated at public expense at Grady Hospital came from that 39% of the population living in substandard areas.

Seventy-two per cent of all juvenile delinquency cases were found to be children living in blighted areas. Fifty-nine per cent of police cases (exclusive of traffic offenses) were made against people who call the slum areas home.

On the basis of these discoveries, business men interested in more economical government, citizens interested in improving social conditions, set out to remedy the situation. These groups felt that the root of the problem lay in the slums. Such a series of facts cannot be mere coincidence. And while there was no assurance that transferring families from bad houses to good ones would reduce crime, fire, and disease, the fact that social evils and poor housing conditions were closely allied was sufficiently significant to prompt citizens interested in remedying these ills to clean up the slums.

Because of the large number of substandard houses and because of the belief that slum clearance would improve social conditions, the Housing Authority of the City of Atlanta was established in 1938 to begin eliminating the slums.

Six slum clearance and rehousing developments were proposed. Surveys were made to determine the areas most in need of such developments....

On the basis of these surveys, definite plans for six housing projects were developed. Twelve months ago when the housing authority was barely a year old, most of the groundwork had been laid for the program which is now in full swing. . . .

DOCUMENTS

THE END OF AN ERA - 1961

The year 1961 marked the end of an era in Atlanta's history. William B. Hartsfield, who had led the city for over twenty-three years, through two wars, racial strife, and great urban development, announced his retirement. Today the busy corridors of Atlanta's Hartsfield International Airport represents a fitting tribute to his contributions to the modern metropolis. His valedictory address follows.

Source: Atlanta Constitution, January 3, 1962.

Gentlemen of the Board of Aldermen: Once again we are able to report to the people of Atmanta another year of great progress on all fronts.

Again we have maintained our unparalleled record among large American cities of 23 consecutive years of cash operation, borrowing nothing for current operating expenses, winding up the year with all bills paid, $37,403 saved in cash discounts for prompt payments, and a cash carry-over of $3,589,556.94, the largest in the history of our town. This is not a surplus, but funds which go back into the budget and enable cash operation for another year.

Also in the management of the poeple's money, we have earned for them $577,170 as interest on idle funds, pending payment for authorized appropriations.

The 1961 Hartsfield administration is proud to turn over to our successors a city in strong and healthy financial condition, not only with all bills paid, but with the various departments adequately equipped, new facilities completed in 1961, together with other needed improvements under contract, much of which will be completed this new year.

The year 1961 has witnessed the completion of our magnificent new airport administration building, taxiways, parking lots, service buildings, etc., a great new facility which, with federal contributions, airline and concessionaire contributions, represents over twenty million dollars, dedicated to a greater Atlanta in the jet age.

ADDED FIRE STATION

We have completed another new and modern fire station and have purchased necessary land for police headquarters expansion.

We have widened North Avenue from Piedmont Avenue to Fort Street. We have spent millions for water pollution control, or sewage plants and facilities, and likewise made important enlargements in our water works system.

We have brought to completion in the past year an observation tower for Grant Park and opened beautiful new bear pits and a seal pool, as well as other landscaping work there. Our priceless possession, the Cyclorama, is being provided with the most modern and scientific fire protection system possible, at a cost of over $40,000, which work should be finished this year.

In the field of urban renewal, we are proceeding on schedule and several of our pending projects should be completed during the current year. In this field, there must be provided more funds, either from bonds or some new sources of revenue, if we are to continue this vital improvement program on a large scale.

In the field of employee relations, we have created 209 new positions in 1961, with the recommendation of the Personnel Department, and in order to render better service to a growing city at a cost of $623,454. We have granted $1,322 longevity salary increases at a cost of $235,000, and made 239 salary range adjustments at a cost of $89,464.

During the year 1961 there was expended by your city, including bond funds, over $14,000,000 for capital improvements and new equipment.

PLANS FOR FUTURE

In addition to the many new improvements and facilities constructed and completed during the year 1961, we have made plans, appropriated funds and let contracts for other vital necessities which will see completion, either during this year 1962 or the immediate future.

Among those already under contract are: additional landscape work, including a beautiful fountain for the front entrance of the airport, which should be completed next spring; the Techwood Viaduct, which should see completion by the middle of this year; new greenhouses for Piedmont Park; and a new incineration plant located off Access Road, near the Chattahoochee River. This new garbage burning plant will take care of the needs of our city for another 10 years, and has been so planned as to take care of additional burning units when necessary. This plant was started in December 1961, and should be completed in the year 1963.

During the year 1961, we contracted with Eastern Airlines to finance the erection of a new maintenance building at the airport, already started and which should be completed during the year 1962.

During the year just past, the City of Atlanta agreed with the State Highway Department to light and maintain the new limited access highway running from the main expressway to and by the Atlanta Airport. The Legislature extended our city limits so as to include this right of way into the airport terminal. This improvement, being done by the state with a federal grant, should be completed in about two more years. When completed it will give Atlanta, with its modern new jet terminal, quick access to downtown and to other points in Georgia, unsurpassed by any other modern terminal in the nation.

TEN-YEAR PLAN ENDS

Incidentally, the year 1961 marks the end of the first 10 years of Atlanta's famous Plan of Improvement, that great governmental overhaul and enlargement, which began with tremendous controversy and opposition, but which has demonstrated its wisdom and soundness over the years. It was this plan which put Atlanta on the road to being a really great city. It was this plan which guaranteed for many more years the growth of the central core city, whose civic health is vital not only to the metropolitan area, but to the entire state. It made, not only for a fairer distribution of taxes and efficient operation of local facilities, but its enlargement of the city limits made for better citizenship. Under it, suburban citizens in all walks of life came in and became active participants, not just helpless spectators. Under this plan, a large body of our most wealthy and influential citizens came into the city. Atlanta has always been fortunate in having its leading and influential citizens participate in its government. This plan made them active voting citizens as well. The beneficent effects of this action have been evident over a period of years and especially in the immediate past when Atlanta needed, as never before, the support of all its good citizens.

Our Department of Building Inspection informs me that during the year 1961 there were 10,158 building permits authorizing $95,849,000 of construction work inside our city limits. Also, during the year 1961, we adopted a new and more modern building code, authorizing many new materials and methods, thus encouraging new and efficient construction. This department informs me that during this new year of 1962, in new public buildings, office buildings, hotels, motels, apartments, warehouses and other types of buildings already planned, Atlanta should really break all existing records.

HAVE MET CHALLENGE

Most certainly we have met the challenge of a growing and dynamic city. About all of these things, we can be truly proud. But after all, they concern only money, manpower and material matters. A real city, in the truest meaning of the word, does not live by these things alone. Accordingly, we have tried to lend support to the cultural affairs of our city—to the performing arts, to exhibitions and good musical entertainment; to the establishment of good places to dine out, to a bright and decent night life, all of which means so much in the attraction of good citizens from elsewhere, and indirectly influences the location of many businesses in out town. A part of this is the new Merchandise Mart, which had the support of the city government, and which itself is a generator of more visitors and more businesses.

We have tried to make our city attractive to those from other parts of the nation having both money to invest and plants to build. It has paid off, both with an influx of new citizens and investments. Atlanta's growing downtown is silent witness to the soundness of our effort to maintain a strong central city, and to attract here the kind of folks who will contribute to our future growth.

But the most important thing about our city, with its natural advantages, as the great Southern regional capital and center of Southeastern trade and commerce, is its good name and its image before the balance of the nation. In this electronic and jet age, no place, no people, and no set of officials can escape the eye and ear of the balance of the world. Nor can they escape their responsibilities as citizens of that world.

MUST LIVE IN PEACE

Science has made all men neighbors, and as such they must find a way to live in peace and without hatred. Great decisions have been made in this field, decisions which have run counter to many of the habits and customs of the old South. Many sections of our southland have tried to stop the inexorable clock of time and progress, but without success and at great cost to themselves.

Atlanta's mature and friendly approach to the problems of racial change has earned for us the respect of the nation. Our leadership has enabled others in the South to do likewise. As the great branch office and regional center of the south, Atlanta's nerves and blood vessels extend all over the nation. To have adopted any other course than racial progress and harmony would have been doubly tragic for us, and a serious blow to our national government in its fight to stave off world communism.

Atlanta's peaceful school desegregation before the eyes of the whole nation was our finest hour. Our great airport terminal, which is our front door, and open to all, regardless of race, color or creed, is evidence to the world of the fact that here is a city which means to be a proud part of the great nation which we must support. Regardless of our personal feelings or past habits, we are living in a changing world, and to progress, Atlanta must be a part of that world.

As I now take leave of the official family with whom I have been associated for 23-1/2 years as mayor, and many more years as a member of your body, please pardon me now for a brief resume: In 1937, I assumed this office, in a city 37 square miles in size, over $3 million in debt, a Police Department in disrepute, and with no budgetary control. Our tax digest was less than $350 million, which included intangibles.

KEPT ON CASH BASIS

Shortly thereafter, we put this city on a cash basis and have kept it there. We reestablished confidence in the Police Department and pride in our city and its civic affairs. We enlisted and have consistently received the support of our business element. We have made our city a center of aviation, improved our court system, installed a modern budget law and raised Atlanta in the estimation of the entire nation. Above all, we have convinced the nation that we are indeed a city too busy to hate, and have thereby increased our own pride and self-respect.

So today I take official leave of a city grown to 138 square miles, a half-million people in its corporate area, a million in the metropolitan area, plus great plants, factories and office buildings, a city on a cash basis for 23 years, efficiently operated, a tax digest of over a billion dollars, a city with pride in itself and high in the estimation of the nation.

Much of this, my fellow workers, has been due to your loyal cooperation and support. No one man could have done it alone. Your team work and your excellent service, together with our fine department heads, has made it possible.

Finally, to the people of Atlanta, those wonderful folks, the like of which there is nowhere else in the nation, goes the major credit. All of the things about which we boast, they made possible with their taxes and their support. For the balance of my life, I will be everlastingly grateful to them for their confidence and support.

And now to the administration of Mayor Ivan Allen, President Samuel Massell, and the newly constituted Board of Aldermen, we offer our support and present to you a city in good condition, with a clean shield.

Thank you, and God Bless our Atlanta!

A NEW MAYOR FOR ATLANTA - 1962

Atlanta's "changing of the guard" in 1961 brought Ivan Allen Jr. to the mayor's office. Allen, the son of a business leader, was himself a chamber of commerce president. He led Atlanta through the tumultuous 1960s, and made a record of progress and racial advance that set a standard for America. Allen's program and attitude were set forth in his first inaugural address, January 3, 1962.

Source: The Atlanta Constitution, January 3, 1962.

This is an occasion when the long finger of history passes over us as we mark the end of an era and the beginning of an era.

When Mayor-Emeritus William B. Hartsfield and the Board of Aldermen took over the administration of the city of Atlanta almost a quarter of a century ago, the city was plagued with the problem of poverty. Today, some 25 years after, a new administration begins and this administration today is faced with the problems of prosperity, problems brought on by growth and problems brought on by the choice we must make as to whether we move forward or backward. The one thing we all know is that we cannot stand still. This is the history of business and of cities.

I think we have made the choice. I think we know as few cities know that lack of progress would be more costly than progress. If we do not go forward, we will be forced to pay, but in a different coin . . . we will pay in the coin of unemployment, in the coin of reduced revenue, in fewer services for the citizens and in the coin of a gradual decline of a once great city.

COST OF PROGRESS

Let's look at the other side of the coin and examine the cost of progress, the cost of moving ahead. First, we determine now what are the services we have to increase . . . what are the physical facilities that we must have in order to maintain our stature as a great city . . . then we have to decide how badly we want these things . . . how we go about getting them and how much we are willing to pay.

Let me state here and now that I think the first rule of thumb for any of the things that must be done in Atlanta is this: That in any area where private enterprise can and will undertake a project, this must be done. This must be encouraged and endorsed and expected. Your city administration will enter the picture only when it has determined that private enterprise cannot undertake those services and provide those facilities which Atlanta must have.

There are other areas where we must work for closer cooperation. Metropolitan Atlanta is a city of a million, and, we like to add, a city in a million. It is obvious that we must pool our resources, our planning and in many instances our facilities in working out our problems that are joint problems of the Metropolitan area. Obviously, this applies to the problems that jointly affect our county and our city.

The other important area, and an area of vital importance, is our sincere approach to the state government in a spirit of awareness of our mutual needs and mutual interests. Let me repeat that these are areas which we must approach in a spirit of complete cooperation, recognizing and seeking recognition of that fact that what affects Atlanta, affects the state; and what affects the state, affects Atlanta.

BEST IN SERVICES

Coming closer to our own doors, let me pledge for this administration the closest attention to the welfare of the city employees in order that we may give the people of Atlanta the very best in efficient services.

Let me pledge the continuation of the financial stability of the city government. Let me pledge a new effort at finding new sources of income. Let this administration go on record as saying that we must work towards a more rapid completion of the great expressway system and the perimeter road which surrounds Atlanta.

We must take a new, hard look at the resources we have and see these resources as fulfilling the needs of Atlanta. Let me give you an example of this: South of Atlanta, within a few miles of Five Points is a great tract of land . . . some 240 acres . . . owned by the City of Atlanta and leased to the Southeastern Fair Association. Here is an area that can provide an expansion of public facilities for entertainment . . . stadium parking, amusement park and many other uses. This is an area which could be made into a happy playground for the people of Atlanta and for the thousands of people who visit us.

In the Urban Renewal program we must use the best minds, the best planning and the most concerted efforts so that this program can move as rapidly as possible.

RAPID TRANSIT

In the field of transportation we must concern ourselves with formulating our plans now for a workable rapid transit system, a problem that addresses itself not only to Atlanta but to the Metropolitan area — and we urge our fellow citizens of Metropolitan Atlanta to work towards the solution of this problem.

When we survey the absolute needs of this growing, bustling, thriving, prosperous city, it is obvious that we must, during this administration, have a bond issue, and we must begin now to filter the needs of the city in terms of priority. A bond commission must be appointed and the needs evaluated over a period of months. This will, of course, be a citizens' committee, and it will have the best possible thinking of the elected and the appointed officials of this administration.

I pledge that this administration will give wholehearted support and tangible evidence to the support of the "Forward Atlanta" movement. I stand ready and willing to go personally anywhere and talk to anybody about the superiority of Atlanta and the practical advantages of moving plants, offices, services and people to our city. This is something I know how to do — I was born and bred in this briarpatch!

In the final analysis, you, the citizens of Atlanta, will exercise your right, your judgment and your concern for Atlanta in determining the items of most urgent need for the city.

Let me go into another field which we must review and evaluate. This is the field of human relations. It is in this area that we must face up to the cold, sober fact that in the national and the international scene, we are an extremely necessary factor in the sum of things.

Atlanta's position demands that we recognize and acknowledge the fact that we are no longer merely a small Southern town. Whatever doubtful comfort we may have had when we were small is gone. What we do and how we do it affects the United States and its place in the world.

Atlanta has by its reputation become one of the legends of the South and of the nation, a legend of progressiveness and a legend of what happens to a city that is determined to move forward in the direction of progress. We are a legend that has become real in our own lifetime. This is one of our greatest assets. This asset we have inherited, and this asset we must not lose.

If I had ever doubted our importance in the scheme of things, if I needed reassurance as to our place in the sun, such doubts would have been dispelled during my trip to Berlin where I had the privilege of representing our city. I talked with the 22 other mayors who had been selected to represent their cities and the United States in a foreign country at the request of the State department. I know how Atlanta is held in the eyes of this country and in the eyes of the world.

MUST BE UNITED

It was in Berlin that the tragic and dramatic lesson of what happens to a divided city came home to me, and if I could make you see it as I saw it, you would share with me my feeling that Atlanta must not be a city divided.

If we are to achieve our true greatness, if we are to fulfill our destiny as not only one of the great cities of the nation, but one of the great cities of the world, we must be a city united, joined by mutual problems and mutual determinations to solve these problems.

This means that as citizens concerned with our city, we must more actively participate in our city government.

I have a growing belief that this new era we are entering into will be one in which people will look to their city government in many ways and for many things, but I have a profound conviction that this WILL be, and MUST be, an administration where there will be an increasing effort on the part of the city government to look to the citizens for more and more participation in areas where the city government does not reach.

Let me give you an example of what I am talking about. There are approximately 50,000 illiterates in metropolitan Atlanta . . . 50,000 people who cannot dial a telephone . . . cannot read a street sign . . . cannot communicate with friends or relatives except verbally.

I see this as a waste of human resources with which the community should concern itself. Early in this administration, I am calling a mayor's conference of citizens to explore the means of attacking this problem in terms of community participation. I am hoping that we can set a target date on which we can say that we have eliminated this problem, that we have salvaged a part of our population in terms of lowering our problem of unemployment, of juvenile delinquency or people on welfare rolls and other dependents of the city and county.

This is something the city administration has no funds for, but it can be done with the help of citizens, concerned citizens. I see this pattern of citizen participation repeating itself in all areas of our city.

BUILD A TRADITION

I say that we begin now to build a tradition of citizen participation in Atlanta and that we build this tradition so that it becomes a part of the heritage of every child who is born in Atlanta and every child who moves to Atlanta.

We must begin now . . . to make our plans, and these plans must be made in the light of our belief in the future of Atlanta, in its potentialities and its destiny. We must determine what we want and how badly we want it. We must begin now to determine how soon we must have a bond issue to provide those things which Atlanta must have in the near future and what we must have in the more distant future.

I ask the help of, first, the Board of Alderman in determining the needs of Atlanta. I ask immediately that the Committee on Municipal Buildings and Athletics survey and determine the facilities which Atlanta must have for an auditorium-coliseum complex that will not only meet the competition of other progressive cities, but will provide those facilities for entertainment, athletic events and recreation which the people of Atlanta must have.

I ask the help of each and every citizen of Atlanta. I ask your confidence, I ask your cooperation, I ask your participation. I pledge to you the best administration I am capable of...

THE CHALLENGE OF THE SEVENTIES - 1970

Mayor Allen led Atlanta through the challenges of the "urban crisis" and racial animosity which have bedeviled recent American history; his administration produced a new Atlanta, one whose spirit typified a new South. Some maintained that Peachtree Street had become Main Street for the entire South. Allen also fostered a growing sense of metropolitanism which many planners believe may be the only viable answer to the crisis of America's cities.

Source: Planning Atlanta, 1970, (Atlanta, 1970).

In the decade starting in 1850, Atlanta was transformed from little more than a hamlet with 2,572 people, to a bustling, growing community of almost 10,000. By the turn of the century, 89,872 people resided in Atlanta. Now, seventy years later, Atlanta has become the home of over a half a million people and the hub of a metropolitan area with a population of over 1,300,000.... In the 1950's, Atlanta's population increased 47% almost completely by annexation. Population growth has since tapered off to a modest increase of 14,871 during the 1960's.

With Atlanta serving as the magnet, the Atlanta metropolitan area steadily increased in population from 214,693 people in 1900 to over 1,302,000 in 1969. The post-World War II movement from central cities to suburban areas in addition to general in-migration shifted the emphasis of metropolitan growth. This trend in metropolitan area growth compared to that of the City of Atlanta continues at a ratio of 19-1. This is caused by the availability of developable residential land in the five-county metropolitan area compared to the scarcity of vacant land for residential use within the city limits. Much of the metorpolitan area gain has been derived from the decline of the agricultural economy in rural areas of the south.

Within Atlanta, the average age of the population is declining due to in-migration of young adults and a growing non-white population. White out-migration from the city has occurred in virtually all age brackets with the heaviest outflow among children and persons in their thirties. The exception appears to be people in their early twenties, for whom the city holds a strong attraction. Non-white migration to Atlanta, which occurs in all age groups under 45, is largely drawn from rural portions of the south and the metropolitan area. Income patterns vary within the city from area to area, but one definite trend is very apparent. Lower income families tend to concentrate in areas around the Central Business District where health and welfare services and facilities are centralized. The moderate and affluent areas lie farther out. The most prosperous areas are located in the northern portions where median household incomes range from two to four times the city-wide average.

During the last decade, Atlanta lost 35,000 of its white population and gained 50,000 non-white. With these populations shifting in and out, Atlanta at present appears to be headed toward becoming a city of extremes, the young and old, the rich and poor. If present trends continue, it will also become more non-white...

Because an urban population needs so many things immediately and on a continuing basis, the foremost requisite of a good physical improvement program must be "balance." No one function of a city should be developed to the detriment or exclusion of others. The same can be said of all component areas which, collectively, form the City of Atlanta.

Such balance is only possible on a total or city-wide basis, as the relative priority item in one area may be low prority in another area. True balance can only be achieved by careful programming over many years.

It has been projected that the 1983 population of the City of Atlanta would be 670,000 or an increase of 33.4 percent over 1969. Such an increase is based on a corollary increase in employment with 190,000 additional jobs anticipated in business and service activities and 20,000 in industry. This growth of population and employment must bring with it of this new development will take place on land which is presently vacant. Other developement will be a conversion of existing uses, most often to more intensive uses.

There is no reason to expect that the accomodation of this growth will require extensive or fundamental changes in the land use pattern. An increased amount of land will be required, but the basic strcture of the present city will be the matrix of the future structure...

The city plan and, hence, the desired ultimate development involves three basic parts: land use, the transportation system and community facilities (schools, parks, public buildings and utilities).

The established pattern of land use must be continued. Vacant and under-developed residential land is expected to develop slowly in relation to economic feasibility....

The ultimate development should include an increased provision for open space, neighborhood parks adjacent to schools and community parks. The use of flood hazard areas for public open space is also proposed.

Some provision has been made for the limitation of strip commercial development, although this is extremely hard to do. All aspects of the city are better served when major streets are relieved of the congestion and confusion of on-street parking serving a commercial strip. Better design standards related to property access, paving, lighting, sign control and landscaping could do much to improve the present situation.

A better solution must be explored which will better relate surrounding office-business and apartment developments to shopping centers. Commercial centers should relate to adjacent neighborhoods, as the Central Business District relates to the city and the region.

A strong Central Business District is needed to provide a focal point and to balance the shopping and business centers in outlying areas....

The final aspect of ultimate development is that of community facilities, including the broad range of schools, parks, public buildings and utilities. These are required to service the multiple operations involved in urban life. Community facilities are expensive and must be assembled as a system over many years. Their adequacy and the level of service to be provided demand intelligent planning and careful programming to serve an urban population...

THE FUTURE OF ATLANTA-1974

In January, 1974 a new Charter for Atlanta went into effect: among its innovations were an eighteen member Council and a decentralized educational system. But more important was the fact that Atlanta, a "New international city" and the "Hub of the South", had elected, and was about to inaugurate, its first black Mayor. Maynard Jackson's Inaugural address recognized that the nation would closely watch as Atlanta fought for its future.

Source: <u>New York Times</u>, January 8, 1974.

Tonight we come together for a very special purpose. This inauguration is more than just the positive reaffirmation that all Atlantans' can work together for the good of the city. This affirmation is symbolized by the very nature of the inaugural program. Conceived, planned and executed by our citizens, this inaugural program brings together two important cultural traditions....

In another and perhaps more important sense, tonight's inaugural symbolizes the full citizen participation which will be the style and the realty of this new administration. Tonight we are witnessing a "People's Inauguration." Over the next four years we shall work to create a people's administration, one that will afford even the poorest and most destitute person an alternative to agony. No longer will we necessitate Langston Hughes' plaintive cry of the masses,

"I swear to the lord I still can't see why
Democracy means everybody but me."

Your presence here is also a <u>strong</u> indication of your renewed faith in the electoral process. It is a <u>strong</u> indication of your hope for our future as a united city. Your presence is a <u>strong</u> indication of your belief in the promise of positive social and political change.

Such faith and hope indeed have become part of what is known as the "Atlanta Style." We use the Hartsfield slogan, "A City too Busy to Hate," but equally as important, we must ask during the difficult days ahead, are we a city too busy to love? That is no mere rhetorical question. For if we are to make this evening a meaningful beginning, we must make a conscious decision to start to change the way we live. We must do more than <u>say</u> we are concerned and that we care. We must begin to translate that concern into action, becuase we know that injustice and inequality are not vague and shadowy concepts that have no tangible dimensions. Behind every unjust act and behind all unequal treatment there are conscious decisions made by conscious men and women who choose not to care.

So, we must be a city of love and our definition of love must be a definition of action. Love must be strong economic growth and prosperity for all. Love must be giving the young a voice in city government and restoring their faith in the electoral process. Love must be concern for the welfare of our senior citizens and a renewed committment to make their years productive and rewarding for all of us. Love must be a balanced diet for all of our children. Love must be decent, safe and sanitary housing for all Atlantans. Love must be working to rid a community of the rats that attack babies while they sleep. Love must be a good education available to all who wish to learn. Love must be an open door to opportunity instead of a closed door of despair. Love must be good jobs, equal treatment and fair wages for all working people. Love must be safe streets and homes where our families can be secure from the threat of violence. Love must be a decision to care for the sick, the infirm and the handicapped. Love must be a city filled with people working together to improve the quality of all our lives. Love must be the absence of racism and sexism. Love must be a chance for everybody to be somebody.

To insure a clear reflection of this essential ethic, this administration must place priority upon serving the needs of the masses as well as the classes. The pending reorganization of our city government will be designed to open wide the doors of city hall to all Atlantans and make our city government more responsive to "people needs" and "people problems"....

Instead of falling prey to all the illnesses of urban life in America, Atlanta has the opportunity to lead the way to a new kind of life. It is awesome to consider, but true: We stand a decisive point in History. Everyone knows that the old south is dead forever. But in spite of much propaganda to the contrary, we have not yet seen the birth of a really new south. Now we stand with a choice: We can live as if this were simply the worst of times, as if there were no path for Atlanta save the terrible mistakes of the urban North. Or we can strike out in still uncharted directions. We can become mired in the ruts of other cities, or we can develop an entirely new mural of urban life. If we dare to work, we can become the guides. We can create the new models. We can serve our city, our state, our section and our nation if we are prepared to create a new kind of city based on a new political vision shared in and worked toward by all Atlantans.

This is the task to which I have already set myself, the task I want to share with you. With your help, your prayers, your strength, your wisdom your compassion, you, the council and I together can show the world that here is a city too strong not to fight, too loving not to care, too great to turn away.

Bibliography

The serious student who begins to search into the urban past is often overwhelmed by the colossal amount of documentation produced by out cities. If he studies the twentieth century he will be virtually swamped by reports, records, proceedings, minutes, etc. If the lay citizen were aware of the cost of printing such volumes, a protest movement would rapidly form. Nevertheless, the materials contained in such exotic volumes will keep squads of scholars busy for years. The bibliography that follows, however, is hardly meant for the scholar for it concentrates on secondary materials that should be available through any good reference library. It seeks to help the layman who cares little for dry statistics or formal records of actions, but who would like to discover more about the City of Atlanta.

A Few Points in 1895 about Atlanta. Atlanta, 1895. A chamber of commerce review of the growing city.

Allen, Ivan. Atlanta from the Ashes. Atlanta, 1928. A laudatory review by the leader of "Forward Atlanta" who presented his city "to the executives of American Business."

The Atlanta Spirit. Altitude and Attitude. Atlanta, 1948.

Allen, Jr., Ivan. Mayor: Notes on the Sixties. New York, 1971. The reminiscences, written with the aid of Paul Hemphill, of an activist mayor who presided over Atlanta's coming of age.

"An Advertising Campaign against Segregated Vice", The American City, IX (July, 1913).

Andrews, Sidney. The South since the War. Boston, 1866.

A Pattern of Progress, Atlanta Model Cities Program. Atlanta, 1969.

A Report of Public School Facilities for Negroes. Atlanta, 1944.
An indictment of the city school system done by the National Urban League.

Atlanta, A City of the Modern South. New York, 1942. Part of the American Guide Series and quite valuable.

Atlanta and Georgia Portrayed. Atlanta, 1885. Largely useful for statistics of city growth since 1880.

Atlanta as the Southeastern Center of Commerce and Finance. Atlanta, 1914. A summary statement, compiled by the chamber of commerce, that emphasizes Atlanta's regional role and why it was awarded the Federal Reserve Bank for the Southeast.

Atlanta: A twentieth Century City. Atlanta, 1904.

Atlanta Centennial Year Book, 1837-1937. Atlanta, 1937.

Atlanta Exposition and South Illustrated. Chicago, 1895. A guide to the great Cotton Exposition of 1895 with many fine photographs.

"Atlanta Massacre", The Independent, LXI (October, 4, 1906).

Atlanta. Past, Present and Future. Atlanta, 1883.

Atlanta Region Comprehensive Plan: Rapid Transit. Atlanta, 1961.

Atlanta: Transportation. Atlanta, 1973. The most recent statistics documentating Atlanta's claim to be "the hub of the South."

Atlanta University Publications. New York, 1968. The Arno Press reprint of twelve studies assesing the problems of the urban black at the turn of the century.

Avery, Isaac Wheeler. The History of Georgia from 1850 to 1881. New York, 1881.

Avery, Myrta Lockett. Dixie after the War . . . New York, 1906.

Bacote, Clarence Albert. The Story of Atlanta University. Atlanta, 1969.

Baker, Harry Givens. Rich's of Atlanta, The Story of a Store since 1867. Atlanta, 1953.

Barker, Meta. "Some High Lights of the Old Atlanta Stage" Atlanta Historical Bulletin, III (January, 1928).

Barnett, Johnathan. "John Portman. Atlanta's One Man Urban Renewal Program", Architectural Record, v. 139 (January 1966.)

Barnwell, V.T. Atlanta City Directory and Stanger's Guide. Atlanta, 1867.

BIBLIOGRAPHY

Baylor, Henry B. Atlas of Atlanta. Atlanta, 1894.

Bisher, Furman, Miracle in Atlanta. Cleveland, 1966. The story of Atlanta's bid for and acquisition of a major league baseball team.

Bowen, J.W.E. (ed.). Addresses and Proceedings of the Congress on Africa...of Gammon Theological Seminary, December 13-15, 1895. Atlanta, 1896.

Boylston, Elise Reid. Atlanta: Its Lore, Legend, and Laughter. Doraville, Georgia, 1968.

Brawley, Benjamin. History of Morehouse College. Atlanta, 1917.

Brittain, Marion Luther (ed). Semi-Centennial History of the Second Baptist Church of Atlanta, Georgia. Atlanta, 1904.

_____. The Story of Georgia Tech. Chapel Hill, N.C., 1948.

Bullock, Henry Morton. A History of Emory University. Nashville, 1936.

Burton, Eldin. "The Metropolitan Opera in Atlanta", Atlanta Historical Bulletin, V (January-April-October, 1940.)

Calhoun, F. Phinizy. "The Founding and the Early History of the Atlanta Medical College." Georgia Historical Quarterly, V (March, 1925).

Candler, Charles Howard. Asa Griggs Candler. Atlanta, 1950.

Carney, Robert. What Happened at the Atlanta Times. Atlanta, 1969. The story of what went wrong in the creation and death of an urban newspaper.

Carter, E.R. The Black Side: A Partial History . . . of the Negro in Atlanta, Georgia. Atlanta, 1894.

Carter, III, Samuel. The Siege of Atlanta, 1864. New York, 1973. For the general reader, and often inaccurate in details.

Cate, Wirt A. (ed.). Two Soldiers: The Campaign Diaries of Thomas J. Key, C.S.A. . . . and Robert J. Campbell, U.S.A. . . . Chapel Hill, N.C., 1938.

Chaney, George Leonard. "The New South-Atlanta", New England Magazine, V (November, 1891).

"Cities of Georgia-Atlanta", Harpers Weekly, XLVII (October, 10, 1903).

City Builder. Atlanta, 1916-1930. A chamber of commerce periodical with much valuable information.

City of Atlanta. A Descriptive, Historical and Industrial Review of the Gateway City of the South. Louisville, 1892-93. Part of the World's Fair Series on Great American Cities with good information provided by many Atlantans.

Clarke, Edwin Young. Atlanta Illustrated. Atlanta, 1881. Over 150 illustrations and much information in a volume first published in 1877 and subsequently revised.

Cleaton, J.D. Standard City Guide of Atlanta. Atlanta, 1907.

Community Facilities, City of Atlanta, 1968. Atlanta, 1969.

Cooper, Walter G. The Cotton States and International Exposition and South, Illustrated. Atlanta, 1896.

Official History of Fulton County. Atlanta, 1934. Part of the history of Georgia authorized in 1929, and a good compilation of data.

Coulter, E. Merton. Georgia: A Short History. Chapel Hill, N.C. 1947.

———. The South during Reconstruction, 1865-1877. Baton Rouge, 1947.

Cox, Jacob D. Atlanta. New York, 1882. Volume IX in the Scribner Series on "Campaigns of the Civil War" and still useful.

Cunningham, Cornelia. Atlanta, City of Today: A Sketch-Book. Atlanta 1933.

Dinnerstein, Leonard. The Leo Frank Case. New York, 1968. An excellent book, the best treatment of a tragic affair.

"Dixie Conditions Stir Unionists--Description of Actual Conditions of Atlanta Textile Workers make Delegates Weep," The Textile Worker, III (December, 1914)

Dyer, John P. The Gallant Hood. Indianapolis, 1950.

Edge, Sarah S. Joel Hurt and the Development of Atlanta. Atlanta, 1955. A granddaughter's testimony on the accomplishments of a "master builder".

BIBLIOGRAPHY

Enslow, J.D. and MacDonald, George (Comps). Atlanta Illustrated. A Story of Success. Atlanta, 1900.

Exposition Cotton Mills--Seventieth Anniversary, 1882-1952. Atlanta, 1952.

"Facts and Forecasts 61/83. Atlanta, 1969.

Fairman, Henry Clay. Chronicles of the Old Guard. . . Atlanta, Georgia 1858-1915. Atlanta, 1915.

Garrett, Franklin M. Atlanta and Environs. A Chronicle of its People and Events, 3v. New York, 1954. A vast 2000 page history that is indispensable for the historian, but is flawed by its year-by-year presentation.

Gay, Mary. Life in Dixie during the War, 1861-1865. Atlanta, 1897.

Georgia, A Guide to its Towns and Countryside. Athens, 1940. The WPA guide for the state of Georgia, compiled by dedicated workers.

Georgia Facts in Figures. A Source Book. Athens, 1946.

Gibson, Thomas, "The Anti-Negro Riots in Atlanta.", Harper's Weekly, L (October, 13, 1906.)

Grantham, Dewey W. Hoke Smith and the Politics of the New South. Baton Rouge, 1958.

Green, James L. Metropolitan Economic Republics. A Case Study in Regional Economic Growth. Athens, 1965.

Hamilton, S.A. "The New Race Question in the South", Arena, XXVII (April, 1902.)

Hand Book of the City of Atlanta. Atlanta, 1898.

Harris, Joel Chandler (ed.) Life of Henry Grady. New York, 1890.

Harris, Julia F. (ed.) The Life and Letters of Joel Chandler Harris. Boston, 1918.

Harrison, John M. "The Volunteer Firemen of Atlanta", Atlanta Historical Bulletin, VI (October, 1941).

Hatcher, George (ed.). Georgia Rivers. Athens, 1962. This volume includes a chapter on the Chattahoochee by Ralph McGill.

Hedley, F.Y. Marching Through Georgia. Chicago, 1890.

Hitz, Alex M. A History of the Cathedral of St. Philip. Atlanta, 1947.

Hornady, John R. Atlanta, Yesterday, Today and Tomorrow. Atlanta, 1922. This volume includes a chronology and much valuable information.

"How Atlanta Cleaned Up", The Literary Digest, XLVI (May 3, 1913).

Howell, Clark. History of Georgia. 4 v. Chicago, 1926.

Hunter, Floyd. Community Power Structure. Chapel Hill, N.C., 1953.

Industries and Resources of Georgia: Manufacturing and Mercantile Resources of Atlanta, Georgia. Atlanta, 1883.

Ingersoll, Ernest. "The City of Atlanta", Harper's New Monthly Magazine, v. 60 (December, 1879).

International Cotton Exposition, Atlanta, Georgia, 1881. Report of the Director-General, H.I. Kimball. New York, 1882.

Ivey, John; Demereth, Nicholas J; Breland, Woodrow W. Building Atlanta's Future. Chapel Hill, N.C., 1948. A textbook for use in the public schools of Atlanta.

Jenkins, Herbert. Keeping the Peace. A Police Chief Looks at his Job. New York, 1970. A retrospective view of how the city and its race relations have changed since the author first became a policeman.

Jennings, M. Kent. Community Influential. The Elites of Atlanta. New York, 1964. A sociological analysis of why Atlanta works.

Johnson, Harvey. "Atlanta, the Gate City of the South", The American City, V (July, 1911).

Johnston, James H. Western and Atlantic Railroad of the State of Georgia. Atlanta, 1931.

Key to Atlanta. Atlanta, 1925.

Key, William. Battle of Atlanta and the Georgia Campaign. New York, 1958.

Knight, Lucian Lamar. History of Fulton County, Georgia. Atlanta, 1930.

Knight, Lucian Lamar. Reminiscences of Famous Georgians. Atlanta, 1907-08.

Kurtz, William G. The Atlanta Cyclorama. Atlanta, 1954.

———. Historic Atlanta: A Brief History of Atlanta and its Landmarks. Atlanta, 1929.

1983 Land Use Plan, City of Atlanta. Atlanta, 1969.

Leckie, George G. Georgia: A Guide to its Towns and Countryside. Atlanta, 1954. An expanded version of the WPA Guide of 1940.

Lewis, Lloyd. Sherman, Fighting Prophet. New York, 1931.

Malone, Henry T. "Atlanta Journalism during the Confederacy", Georgia Historical Quarterly, XXXVII (September, 1953).

———. "The Weekly Atlanta Intelligencer as a Secessionist Journal", XXXVII (December, 1953).

Martin, Harold H. Ralph McGill, Reporter. Boston, 1972.

Martin, Stiles A. The State Capitol, A Great Asset to Atlanta. Atlanta, 1948.

Martin, Thomas H. Atlanta and its Builders. A Comprehensive History of the Gate City of the South, 2 vols. (Atlanta, 1902). The books include an excellent biographical section and a long analysis of the Atlanta campaign.

Marx, David. "A History of the Jews of Atlanta", Reform Advocate, (November, 1911).

McBride, R.B. and McDonald, R.S. Atlanta of Today. Atlanta, 1897.

McDonald, T.C. Free Masonry and its Progress in Atlanta and Fulton County. Atlanta, 1925.

McGill, Ralph. A Church, A School. Nashville, 1959. McGill's articles protesting racial injustice. "It is night now in Atlanta, and it may be a long one."

———. Story of the Trust Company of Georgia. Atlanta, 1951.

McMahan, C.A. The People of Atlanta. A Demographic Study of Georgia's

Capital City. Athens, 1950.

Miller, Paul W. (ed.) Atlanta. Capital of the South. New York, 1949.

Mitchell, Eugene. "H.I. Kimball: His Career and Defense", Atlanta Historical Bulletin, III (October, 1938). The best treatment of the Northerner who helped rebuild Atlanta.

Mosely, Clement Charlton. "The Case of Leo M. Frank, 1913-1915". Georgia Historical Quarterly, LI (March, 1967).

New York News Letter, September - October, 1904. An edition of the New York Life Insurance Company's newsletter dedicated to Atlanta - includes many fine photos.

Nixon, Raymond B. Henry W. Grady: Spokesman of the New South. New York, 1943.

Northern, William J. Men of Mark in Georgia. 7 vols. Athens, 1907-1912.

Notable Men of Atlanta and Georgia. Atlanta, 1913.

Now. . . for Tomorrow. Atlanta, 1954. Part of the metropolitan area master plan and more comprehensive than most statistical analyses.

Opportunity for Urban Excellence. Report of the Atlanta Commission on Crime and Juvenile Delinquency. Atlanta, 1966.

Palmer, P.A. (comp.) Seventy-Fifth Anniversary. St. Philips Cathedral, Atlanta, Georgia, 1847-1922. Atlanta, 1922.

Parkes, E.L. History of the First Fifteen Years of Gammon Theological Seminary. Atlanta, 1899.

Pioneer Citizens History of Atlanta, 1833-1902. Atlanta, 1902.

Pittinger, William. Capturing a Locomotive. A History of Secret Service in the Late War. Washington, 1905. An account of the Andrew's Raid by one who survived.

Pierce, Joseph A. The Atlanta Negro, A Collection of Data on the Negro Population of Atlanta, Georgia. Atlanta, 1940.

Planning Atlanta, 1970. Atlanta, 1970.

Plan of Improvement for the Governments of Atlanta and Fulton County, Georgia. Atlanta, 1950. The crucial document that led to rationalization of metropolitan governmental services.

Prince, Margaret. The Negro and the Ballot in the South. Atlanta, 1959.

Prince, Richard E. Steam Locomotives and History. Georgia Railroad and West Point Route. Salt Lake City, 1962.

Proposed Areas for Expansions of Negro Housing in Atlanta. Atlanta, 1947.

Ragsdale, B.D. The Story of Georgia Baptists, Atlanta, 1938.

Rebuilding Atlanta. Atlanta, 1939. The first report of the Municipal Housing Authority.

Reed, Thomas H. (comp.) The Government of Atlanta and Fulton County, Georgia. Atlanta, 1938.

Reed, Wallace P. (ed.) History of Atlanta, Georgia. Syracuse, 1889. Probably the best early history of Atlanta, with over 200 pages of biographical information.

Report of the Forward Atlanta Commission, 1926-1929. Atlanta, 1930. The details of the movement that made Atlanta's national reputation as a progressive southern city.

Report to the City of Atlanta on a Plan for Local Transportation, December, 1924. Atlanta, 1924. New Yorker John Beeler reported on the poor performance of city government.

Rogers, Ernest. The Old Hokum Bucket. Atlanta, 1949. A compendium of human interest articles from the Atlanta Journal, 1943-49.

Rooks, Charles S. The Atlanta Elections of 1969. Atlanta, 1970. Rooks finds that a new black coalition will probably rule Atlanta for the foreseeable future.

Sands, Herbert R. Organization and Administration of the City Government of Atlanta, Georgia. Atlanta, 1912.

Schneider, Franz. A Survey of the Public Health Situation, Atlanta, Georgia. Atlanta, 1913. This and the previous citation were reports done by the New York Bureau of Municipal Research at the request of the chamber of commerce to assess the strengths and weaknesses of city government in

Atlanta.

Sheehan, C.J. "Atlanta Public Schools, 1873-1883," <u>Atlanta Historical Bulletin</u>, II (November, 1936).

Shufelt, Marcia. <u>A Checklist of Atlanta, Georgia imprints from 1846-76 with a historical introduction</u>. Rochestoer, 1958.

Shurter, Edward D. (ed.). <u>The Complete Orations and Speeches of Henry Grady</u>. Norwood, Mass., 1910.

Silbey, Celestine. <u>Peachtree Street, U.S.A.: An Affectionate Portrait of Georgia</u>. New York, 1963

Smith, George G. <u>The Story of Georgia and the Georgia People, 1733-1860</u>. Macon, 1900.

<u>Social and Economic Pattern of Georgia</u>. Atlanta, 1939. Another WPA report done by a competent team.

Stacy, James. <u>History of the Presbyterian Church in Georgia</u>. Elberton, Ga., 1912.

Stokes, Thomas L. <u>Chips off My Shoulder</u>. Princeton, 1940.

Stone, Charles F. <u>The Story of Dixiesteel. The First Fifty Years, 1901-1951</u>. Atlanta, 1951. The epic story of the Atlanta, Atlantic and Atlanta Steel Hoop Combination.

Strozier, Harry. <u>Code of the City of Atlanta of 1942</u>. Atlanta, 1942.

Suddeth, Ruth (ed.). <u>An Atlanta Argosy: An Anthology of Atlanta Poetry</u>. Atlanta, 1938.

Tankersley, Allen. <u>College Life at Old Oglethorpe</u>. Athens, 1951.

Thompson, C. Mildred. <u>Reconstruction in Georgia, Economic, Social, Political, 1865-1872</u>. New York, 1915.

Toombs, Henry J. "City Planning in Atlanta," <u>Landscape Architecture</u>, 43 (April, 1953.).

Train, Arthur. "Did Leo Frank get Justice?" Everybody's, XXXII (March, 1915.).

Tucker, Nana. <u>The Atlanta Music Club Silver Anniversary: History and</u>

Record. Atlanta, 1940.

Vance, Rupert B. and Demerath, Nicolas J. (eds.) The Urban South. Chapel Hill, N.C. 1954.

Viorst, Milton. "Black Mayor, White Power Structure," The New Republic, June 7, 1975.

Von Abele, Rudolph. Alexander H. Stephens, A Biography. New York, 1946.

Welch, N.M. First Annual Report of the Atlanta Chamber of Commerce, for the Year 1885, Historical, Descriptive, Statistical. Atlanta, 1886.

Whitten, Robert. The Atlanta Zone Plan. Atlanta, 1922.

Williams, Eleanor. Ivan Allen. A Resourceful Citizen. Atlanta, 1950.

Williford, William B. Peachtree Street, Atlanta. Athens, 1962. The iconography of Atlanta's main street.

Wilson, John Stainback. Atlanta as it is: Being a Sketch of its Early Settlers. New York, 1871. The best description of Atlanta during the Reconstruction era.

Woodward, C. Vann. Tom Watson, Agrarian Rebel. New York, 1938.

Wright, Wade Hampton. "Georgia Power Company," Atlanta Historical Bulletin, II July, 1938.

INDEX

Aaron, Hank, 74
Abernathy, Ralph, 70
Adair, George W., 23
Adams, C. B., 36
Agnew, Spiro T., 72
Alexander, Dorothy, 53
Alexander, William, 59
Allen, Ivan, Jr., 66-71
Anderson, Marian, 49
Andrews, James, 14, 52
Andrews, M. Neil, 62
Angier, N. L., 26
Arnett, Trevor, 64
Atkinson, Edward, 27
Atkinson, H. M., 40
Austell, Alfred, 17

Baker, Joseph, 4-5
Bard, Samuel, 23
Barry, John, 4
Bartholomay, William, 68
Bartlett, Julia, 31
Beavers, James, 44-46, 48, 50-52, 55
Beckwith, John, 34
Bell, Griffin B., 68
Bernhardt, Sarah, 28
Blank, Morgan, 59
Bomar, Benjamin, 5
Bond, Julian, 66, 69-70
Booth, Edwin, 26
Borglum, Gurzon, 51
Boyd, Mrs. Isaacs, 41
Bragg, Braxton, 14
Brisbane, Albert, 2
Brown, Joseph, 11, 37
Brown, Julius, 26
Brown, Mack H., 56
Brumby, Thomas, 39
Buell, William, 6
Bullock, Rufus, 20, 23, 27
Butt, William H., 8

Calhoun, James, 14-17, 19, 25

Calhoun, John C., 4
Calhoun, William L., 26-27
Candler, Asa, 32, 35, 41, 46-49, 51, 53
Carlisle, Julia, 3
Carmichael, Stokley, 69-70
Carter, Jimmy, 72, 74-75
Caruso, Enrico, 48
Clarke, R. M., 18
Clement, Rufus E., 70
Cleveland, Grover, 30, 32, 36
Cobb, Howell, 7, 20
Collier, Charles, 32, 37
Collier, George W., 3
Cone, Earl, 46
Cone, Francis, 5
Cook, Rodney, 71
Cooper, James, 20
Cooper, J. T., 32
Carrie, Arthur, 47
Crane, Benjamin, 22
Crisp, William, 9
Cutter, Howard, 49

D'Alvigney, Noel, 16
Daniel, D. G., 5
Davis, Jefferson, 13, 31
DeGive, Lawrence, 21, 26, 35, 49
Dobbs, Samuel, 49
Douglas, Stephen A., 13
Doyle, Alexander, 35
DuBois, W. E. B., 37, 41

Eagan, John, 45, 59
Eaves, Reginald, 74-75
Edwards, H. Griffith, 66
Eisenhower, Dwight D., 63
English, James, 26-28
Ezzard, William, 10-14, 21-22

Felton, William H., 25

Ferrar, Geraldine, 43, 49
Ferst, M. A., 51
Fillmore, Milliar, 8, 10
Finch, Tom, 56
Formwalt, Moses, 5
Fowler, Wyche, 73
Frank, Leo, 45-47
Fuller, Steve, 70

Gaston, Ike, 58
Gibbs, G. T., 7
Gilbert, Bradford, 38
Gilbert, Joshua, 4-5
Gilmer, George R., 1
Glenn, John, 10
Glenn, John T., 33
Glenn, Luther, 11, 13, 16
Goodwin, George, 60
Goodwin, John B., 29, 35
Gordon, John, 28, 38, 42
Grady, Henry, 23, 26, 30-31, 34-35, 59
Grant, Lemuel P., 3, 15, 29
Graves, John, 40
Gress, George, 33, 38
Griffin, Eli, 18

Hallinan, Paul, 67
Hambleton, James P., 12
Hammock, Cicero C., 24-25
Hammond, Dennis F., 22
Hancock, Walker, 72
Harding, Warren G., 50
Harris, Joel C., 26-27, 43
Harrison, Benjamin, 34
Hartsfield, William B., 34 51, 56-66
Hayes, Rutherford B., 26
Heisman, John, 41
Helme, William, 9
Hemphill, William A., 34
Hendersen, Alice, 74

Herndon, Alonzo, 29, 41, 59
High, Mrs. Joseph M., 52
Hill, Benjamin, 20, 29, 31
Hillyer, George, 30
Hoge, Edward, 29
Hood, John B., 16
Hornady, Henry, 17
Howard, David T., 48
Howell, Clark, 36, 38, 56
Howell, Evan, 26, 40
Hughes, Columbus, 8
Hulsey, William, 20
Humphries, Charner, 1
Hunt, John, 4
Hurt, Joel, 25, 29, 31-34, 37, 39, 45, 51, 58

Inman, John, 74
Inman, Samuel M., 19, 28, 41, 46
Ivy, Hardy, 1

Jackson, Maynard, 57, 71, 73-75
Jackson, Mr. Maynard, 65
Jacobs, Joseph, 30
Jacobs, Thornwell, 59
James, John, 22-23
Jenkins, Charles, 26
Jenkins, Herbert, 60, 65, 68, 70
Johnson, Andrew, 19
Johnson, Lyndon B., 70
Johnston, Joseph, 15-16
Jones, Bobby, 54
Jones, Thomas, 24
Joyner, William R., 30, 42

Kennedy, John F., 67
Key, James L., 41-42, 48-51, 54-55
Kimball, H. I., 20, 22, 26-27, 29-30
King, Lonnie, 65

INDEX

King, Martin Luther, Jr., 53, 66, 68, 70-71, 74
King, Mrs. M. L., Sr., 74
King, Porter, 37
Kleinbaker, Barney, 35

Lamar, L. Q. C., 47
Lautier, Lous, 64
LeGraw, Roy, 55, 58-59
Leyden, A., 5
Lincoln, Abraham, 17
Lindsey, Archie, 64
Long, Stephen, 2
Longstreet, James, 31
Lowe, Thomas, 14
Lowry, W. M., 18
Lukeman, Augustus, 51

Maddox, Lester, 64, 66-68, 72
Maddox, Robert, 43
Mallon, Bernard, 23
Markham, William, 8, 11-12, 25, 37
Marshall, Thomas, 49
Marye, P. T., 41
Massell, Benjamin, 64
Massell, Sam, 71-73
McDaniel, Ira, 9
McDaniel, J. O., 5
McDaniel, P. C., 5
McGill, Ralph, 53, 65, 71
McKinley, William, 38
McPherson, James, 16, 22, 28, 33
Meade, George, 19
Medina, Ernest, 72
Mikell, Henry, 48
Mims, John T., 7-8
Mims, Livingstone, 39-40
Mims, Mrs. Livingstone, 31
Mitchell, Margaret, 56-57, 59, 62

Montgomery, J. M. C., 1

Nelson, Allison, 9
Newman, Allen, 44
Norcross, Jonathan, 3, 6, 12, 26, 28

Ogilby, T. S., 7
O'Neill, James, 7
O'Reilly, Thomas, 16, 60
Ottley, John, 55

Paderewski, Ignace Jan, 39
Palmer, Charles, 57-58
Parkins, William H., 21
Patterson, Eugene, 65, 69
Patterson, Jack, 70
Paxon, Frederick, 46
Pemberton, John S., 31-32
Peters, Richard, 10
Phagan, Mary, 45
Polk, Leonidas, 15
Pope, John, 19
Portman, John, 64, 66, 70, 75
Powell, Thomas, 27
Preacher, G. Lloyd, 54

Ragsdale, Isaac N., 52-54
Reed, Thomas Harrison, 57, 62
Rich, Morris, 19, 51-52
Ridge, John, 2
Roach, E. J., 29
Roesch, Charles, 29
Roosevelt, Franklin D., 55-56, 60
Roosevelt, Theodore, 41
Root, Sidney, 31
Ryan, Matthew, 29

Salm-Salm, Felix, 17
Schofield, Louis, 11
Scott, William A., 53
Seeley, F. L., 42
Sellers, Cleveland, 70
Selznick, David, 58

Seymour, Horatio, 20
Sherman, Thomas, 42
Sherman, William T., 3, 15-16, 27, 31-32
Simpson, Leonard, 6
Sims, Walter, 50-51
Slaton, John, 46
Slayton, W. F., 27
Smith, Francis P., 53
Smith, Hoke, 32, 36, 42
Smith, Jasper, 33
Smith, Muggsy, 68
Spencer, Samuel B., 24, 26
Stanley, Henry, 34
Stephens, Alexander, 5, 13, 25
Stevenson, Adlai, 63
Styles, Cary, 20
Sunday, Billy, 48

Taft, William Howard, 43, 48-49
Tallmadge, Eugene, 60
Thompson, J. Edgar, 1, 3
Thompson, Joseph, 4
Thrasher, John, 2-3
Toombs, Robert, 20
Torras, Raymond, 50
Torrey, Annie C., 23

Vandiver, Ernest, 65
Vincent, Edward, 7

Walker, William, 16, 40
Ward, Horace, 64
Ware, Edmund, 19
Washington, Booker T., 37
Watson, Thomas, 46
West, Thomas, 10
Whitaker, Jared, 10
White, William, 5

Williams, Hosea, 73
Williams, James E., 17-19
Wilson, John, 7
Wilson, Woodrow, 29, 45, 49
Winn, Cortland, 44-45
Winship, Joseph, 8, 30
Wood, Leonard, 36, 48
Woodruff, Ernest, 49, 59, 63
Woodruff, Robert, 51
Woodson, Carter, 47
Woodward, James G., 38, 41-46
Woodward, J. C., 39
Wurm, Ferdinand, 23

Young, Andrew, 73